Scott

GOPHERS AND CHEETAHS

You have what it takes to be an effective leader. Good Luck.

Neil.

GOPHERS AND CHEETAHS

A Faster Way to Small Business Growth

R. Neil Thiessen

iUniverse, Inc.
New York Lincoln Shanghai

Gophers and Cheetahs
A Faster Way to Small Business Growth

Copyright © 2007 by R. Neil Thiessen

All rights reserved. No part of this book may be used or reproduced by any means, graphic, electronic, or mechanical, including photocopying, recording, taping or by any information storage retrieval system without the written permission of the publisher except in the case of brief quotations embodied in critical articles and reviews.

iUniverse books may be ordered through booksellers or by contacting:

iUniverse
2021 Pine Lake Road, Suite 100
Lincoln, NE 68512
www.iuniverse.com
1-800-Authors (1-800-288-4677)

Because of the dynamic nature of the Internet, any Web addresses or links contained in this book may have changed since publication and may no longer be valid.

ISBN: 978-0-595-45571-3 (pbk)
ISBN: 978-0-595-70394-4 (cloth)
ISBN: 978-0-595-89873-2 (ebk)

Printed in the United States of America

The information, ideas, and suggestions in this book are not intended to render professional advice. Before following any suggestions contained in this book, you should consult your personal accountant or other financial advisor. Neither the author nor the publisher shall be liable or responsible for any loss or damage allegedly arising as a consequence of your use or application of any information or suggestions in this book.

Contents

Preface ix
Acknowledgements. xi
Introduction. xiii
Chapter 1   Gophers and Cheetahs. 1
Chapter 2   A conversation with yourself 12
Chapter 3   Deciding to grow 18
Chapter 4   Your business assets. 22
Chapter 5   Skills for growing and getting over the wall. 30
Chapter 6   The Diamond Solution 44
Chapter 7   Opportunity Assessment. 69
Chapter 8   Staffing the small business. 81
Chapter 9   Employee Involvement and the Value of Money 86
Chapter 10 Diamond in the rough. 91

Preface

I have always felt that my career was full and complete. I have been an owner-operator and worked for large corporations. I feel I have experienced it all—the good, bad, and ugly—in the business world. Starting and running my own business was not even on the radar when I completed my formal education in Chemical Research Technology at the Southern Alberta Institute of Technology back in the 1960's but something inside me drew me there. During the late 1970's and early 1980's I became a partner in a very successful vegetation management company based in Calgary, Alberta. Being a small business owner was a tremendous experience for me. There were many people along the way that helped me learn the subtleties of running and owning a business and I can't thank them enough.

Perhaps the largest challenge I faced during this time was trying to balance my work life with my business life. My experience with this challenge is one of the main reasons I decided to write this book. I wanted to help other small business owners and managers like you understand that you are not alone in your plight and that you can leverage the experiences of others to manifest your business success much more quickly by doing so.

It was at this period in my career that I realized the importance of business discipline. Understanding the relationships between people became my passion as it was evident to me that nothing happens without a commitment from one person to another to take action and deliver a result. Working on and perfecting this discipline grew out of analysis of my own business but it struck me that these interactions happened in every other business too, as well as between any two people outside of a business setting. It is this discipline that I will share with you in this book.

During my busiest years, I found great satisfaction in being an active member of a number of professional and trade associations, including holding senior office positions for international industry organizations. I learned a tremendous amount about leadership and people during this time. My involvement in these organizations taught me a great deal about leading teams, whether these teams consisted of my employees or not.

In addition to numerous awards and recognition for achievement in these organizations, the greatest of all rewards was the tremendous network of friends and business associates I have been fortunate enough to get to know. They have been a source of great pride, inspiration, and joy for many, many years. Anywhere I travel these days I am not far from some of these life-long contacts and I truly appreciate the time I have to spend with them.

My association with fraternal and other organizations, such as the Shriners and Kinsmen Clubs, also influenced me greatly. These organizations exemplify the concept of giving and showed me the true value that a giving society can create.

In my consulting business I have been fortunate enough to have associates that are recognized leaders in their field and who bring the wisdom of their many years of hands-on life and business experiences to task. Their knowledge, experience, and giving personalities create tremendous value for our clients.

This book is inspired by my desire to help small business owners and managers reduce the pain in growing their business and at the same time open up the world of unseen opportunity and potential. I trust you will gain insight into your own business and hope that you leverage what I have written about into ridiculous success.

My sincere desire is that my experiences can, in some way, save you frustration, time, and money. I hope that you find value in these pages, for if you do, you will have helped to make my dreams come true. My success is your success. If I can be of service to you please visit www.ableconsulting.ca.

Acknowledgements

This book would not have been possible without the 45 years of love and patience of my wonderful wife Eileen. Her steadfast support of my career and my many business adventures has helped to make me who I am and for that I am forever grateful. I also acknowledge my three children: Colin, Shannon, and Jason, without whom I would not have learned most of what I know. Special thanks also to their spouses: Cindy, Kevin, and Isabelle, respectively, for their ongoing support and inspiration.

This book would also not have been possible without the support of my business partners and associates: Dwayne and Nancy Neustaeter, Charlie Purfeerst, Bob Black, Barney Palmer, Dr. Phil Charlton, and Ray Cullen. Special thanks to all of you and especially to my son Jason for helping my dream become a reality. You have helped to extract what has been rattling around in my mind for the past six years and I can't thank you enough. I would be remiss if I didn't also thank my many consulting clients for allowing me the opportunity to live my passion. I trust you have received as much from me as I have from you.

It was my parents, Roy and Miriam Thiessen, who instilled in me the values that I have carried with me my entire life, and for them I have saved the greatest acknowledgement. Although they are no longer with me they continue to inspire me to live these values every single day of my life. The most important thing they ever taught me was to be a giver in life, not a taker. I practiced this value throughout my business life and also through my association with the Kinsmen Clubs, the Shriners, and other volunteer organizations. My parents gave of themselves their entire lives and set a standard I strive to live up to. It gave them a great source of self-satisfaction and joy and it offers me the same.

Giving of your time and energy is crucial to a successful and meaningful life and I encourage you to give as much as you can.

Best Wishes,

Neil
August 2007

Introduction

I envy you, the entrepreneur, as a small business owner or manager because you have one of the best "jobs" there is. The decisions you make have direct and immediate impact on your financial well-being and that of any number of employees. Your behaviour dictates the temperature in the room. Your communication and negotiation skills determine how people feel about you and how they interact with your company. Your ability to exhibit leadership and inspire others to do great things impacts everyone in your sphere. You are on the cusp of significant growth and you have the power to get yourself and your business to the Promised Land. Now, that's exciting stuff. Of course, that can be a little scary as well.

That's where I come in. As a small business consultant my role is to help you maneuver through the landmines of growth and work with you to get over the wall. In the pages that follow I have attempted to distill some of the major topic areas and business domains that I work on with my consulting clients. My goal is to offer you meaningful concepts and tools that you can use to manifest positive change in your business. I apologize up front for not being able to relay to you the depth of these topics that I would like but if I did so you would be walking around with a three thousand page book right now.

This book is about how to put business discipline into running your day-to-day operation and getting clarity about where you are and where you want to be. Using the approaches outlined in this book you will hopefully accomplish what I have personally seen many small business owners do—achieve extraordinary results. I will summarize several key success factors to attaining these results and will offer powerful and practical tools that can change your business, and your life.

Over the course of the next 10 chapters I am going to bring you through a series of topic areas that I have found to be critical to the success, or failure, of small businesses. First, you'll check in with yourself as to what is going on in your life and business. From there you will walk through a conversation about why you want to improve or change what is going on in your business. Once you are clear on whether growth is the right option you will have an opportunity to take an inventory of your company's existing assets. I will also discuss some of the skill sets that you will need in your company in order for you to take it to the next level. You need to assess if you have the skills in your organization or if you need to seek help or coaching.

Once you have looked at some key skills for survival and growth, I will introduce you to the Diamond Solution in Chapter 6. This powerful tool will make visible what is currently working in your business and what is not. As you become familiar with its use, and the interpretations it allows, you will begin to see how it can be used to fix what is broken, investigate new opportunities, and literally see your business pictorially laid out in front of you.

I have tested the Diamond Solution in many different industries and scenarios and have found that once small business owners start to use it, and understand the empowerment it gives them and their employees, the magic starts to happen. The magic is simple, and it's called *business discipline*. The Diamond Solution often uncovers many unseen opportunities for your business. In Chapter 7 I'll introduce you to Opportunity Assessment, a way of managing these opportunities.

I will then review with you in more detail issues related to staffing small businesses and ensuring that you have the right people in place to move your organization forward. A key element to the success of small business, or any sized business for that matter, is the development of trust between owners and the employees who do the work that delivers value to the organization and its customers. Trust manifests itself in business in the form of involvement and I will provide you an important example of how the value of money relates to this involvement.

The tenth and final chapter is really a brief story provided by one of my consulting clients who has experienced incredible growth thanks to the tools and practices I introduce in this book. This story provides highlights of the kind of growth and development that is possible in business when owners and managers are open-minded, engaged, and looking for ways over the wall.

CHAPTER 1

Gophers and Cheetahs

I have chosen the title *Gophers and Cheetahs* because they represent two completely opposing images to me—particularly as it relates to business. Both animals exist in the wild and both have and can exist with humans in their environment. This trait shows their adaptability—a critical element for business success. It is clear though, that they prefer to be left alone in their natural environment as they flourish without the interference or influence of humans.

Upon closer examination, their similarities are few. The gopher, sometimes known as the Richardson Ground Squirrel, is a cute, furry little animal that lives primarily on the ground and in its burrowed holes. While it cannot tolerate light in its underground environment, it does spend much of its day above ground sunning itself as it goes about the business of foraging on roots and tubers, often dragging above-ground plants underground into its burrow.

Many businesses operate like a colony of gophers. Day-to-day business seems to be taken care of and life appears to be going along smoothly. However, when there is any sign of danger the gopher quickly finds a convenient hole to run and hide in. Often when they try to fight an enemy threat they are simply overpowered because of their size. And as bright as they are they often get confused and distracted and end up trying to cross busy roads—many ending up run over. They simply lose their familiar surroundings and become victims.

In contrast to the gopher, the cheetah eats small animals and runs down his prey by leaping on it. Because it is the fastest mammal on earth it creates opportunities to feed itself and its family. With an acceleration speed of 70 miles per hour (112 km/hr) and a chase speed of 45 miles per hour (72 km/hr), a gazelle, its preferred meal, has little chance of avoiding capture.

By design, the cheetah is built for speed and agility, thus making it very competitive in the wild. Large nostrils and lungs provide quick air intake; its large liver, heart, and adrenals also facilitate a rapid physical response. A long fluid body helps lengthen its stride. The long tail acts as a rudder to facilitate sharp-angled turns during pursuit. The retinal fovea is elongated to provide a wide-angled view of the world and the tear marks under the eyes provide a defense against the powerful reflection of the sun.

The cheetah has few natural predators because of its quickness and ability to change direction and stay focused on what is important to its survival. In many ways they are similar to our domestic house cat: they purr, hiss, and growl, yet they have been able to survive for over four million years on earth.

So why did I pick these two animals to compare to business? It's really quite simple. The question is: do you want to have a business that is comfortable and laid back but when there is any sign of danger or threat, it retreats into a hole? Or worse, have it flee in any random direction only to end up being run over? On the other hand, do you want to create a business that is energetic, flexible, streamlined, and powerful? Do you want a business that can change direction quickly yet stay focused on the goal at hand?

I wish for you to be the cheetahs in the business world. This requires that you and your organization become focused, adaptable, flexible, and efficient. I want you to be prepared to pounce on opportunities as they appear without the fear that every decision may be a disaster.

If you master the fundamentals of business, you will survive and flourish over time. It is all right to be the hunted, but you need to give yourself permission to prepare for long term growth and survival.

If you are serious about stabilizing and growing your business I am confident you will find the material in this book helpful in attaining this goal. I do recommend that you read a few chapters at a time and let the material digest. This is especially true of Chapter 6 about the Diamond Solution, as it is something that I want you to embrace and implement into your company culture.

Running a business and what you do when you hit the wall

I never intended to be a business consultant when I retired. In fact I didn't think I would ever have time to commit to a business venture of any kind. My plan was to relax while spending my winters in Arizona golfing and doing glass fusion and woodwork and my summers in Western Canada, relaxing at the lake.

What this past number of years has taught me is that we are a resilient society, full of many ethnic and social cultures and most importantly, we cherish our way of life. The way of life and the standard of our existence here in North America is largely due to the innovation of the people and the opportunities that exist.

Because small businesses play such a large role in Canadian society, (approximately 94% of Canada's 2.4 million businesses have 19 or fewer employees) it is important that we remember that these small businesses are made up of people, approximately five million of them[1]. And it is the interaction of people that allows us to get things done. It is the action taken and the results produced that will ultimately determine if a business simply exists or grows and expands.

Yes, there is an element of luck, timing, and circumstance that can determine if a small business even exists, or whether it grows and is sustainable. However, the entrepreneurial spirit and effort of ordinary people drive these ventures and small businesses.

Many small businesses start out with one or two individuals deciding that they want to venture on their own with the hope and dream that they will be able to grow and have a stable and sustainable business to provide them and their employees with a safe and secure future. Many do not realize this dream as they become disheartened, financially disoriented, or simply tired of the long hours required to start and run a small business.

One thing is for sure, almost all small start-up businesses have great intentions and expectations in the beginning. Nobody starts a business with the expectation that in several years they will fail, or become disheartened and give up. Small business owners start off knowing that there will be challenges and that they will have to work hard to be successful. But, often they do not realize that somewhere in the start-up and growing years they will hit the proverbial "wall".

You know when you have hit the wall when:

- You find that you are working harder and harder and not solving problems

---

1. Statistics Canada, July 2005.

- You are frustrated because you can't find committed people
- Your days are long and your profits are not expanding at the same rate
- Your equity is always in jeopardy
- Your marriage or relationships are strained because of the business pressures
- You can't get clarity on where you are and what is going wrong
- You can't see the future clearly
- You're too busy with today's details so have little opportunity to see or act on business growth opportunities
- You're about ready to dump the business and go back to work for someone else

I have personally experienced at least a little of each and every one of the indicators above. I hit the wall a few times in my career and learned from each experience. The entrepreneurial spirit that drives us into our own businesses is not a spirit we give up easily. Rather we fight it and bang our head against the wall, trying to survive and create the future we envisioned. While we can pursue this path of frustration and distraction, an alternative is to take action and get resolved about the future for yourself, your family, and your employees.

From my observations, the common threads that most small businesses have in common during their growth are: committed owners, a desire to grow so they can provide stable employment and opportunity for employees, and a desire to create a future nest egg where they can either leave the business knowing it is in good hands and that it will provide a sustainable retirement income or sell the company.

I won't spend much time on the financial aspects of your small business, but rather on human interaction that produces results. While I recognize that financial viability is critical, I want to emphasize the human side, as it ultimately will determine if you are successful or not.

I am a firm believer that all businesses can significantly improve their efficiency, effectiveness, and therefore profitability by instilling the business discipline that I describe in the Diamond Solution in Chapter 6. Imagine what it would be like if everyone did what they said they would do, on time, every time. The small businesses that I consult to have become more flexible, more disciplined, and more focused on their goals. They have a greater ability to adapt and change than ever before. This is not because of anything that I do, but rather because they are becoming more disciplined in how they interact with each other to produce better quality products and services to satisfy their customers.

One of my clients recently told me that the business discipline of accountability delivered by the Diamond Solution significantly helped him in his business. He now has confidence that his employees are more than capable of making and managing their commitments to each other to the extent that he can leave the business for days at a time and not worry like he used to. This is a huge statement for a small business owner who previously felt he needed to be there all the time.

Once a business has clarity on what is working and what is not, amazing opportunities begin to unveil themselves. The business owners and managers I work with gain confidence with this clarity to move forward into unfamiliar territory with renewed energy and ambition. The cheetah in them comes to life and they become focused on what is truly possible in their business.

The customer

While I talk in this book about you and your staff and a lot of internal issues, NEVER forget the reason for your existence in business: the CUSTOMER. Everything you do or produce must be to create satisfied customers. If your organization is not focused on producing a satisfied external customer, beware. Customers, the people that pay the bills, are keys to your success. I cannot stress enough the importance of customer retention in our very competitive world.

While we don't hear as much about customer satisfaction as we used to, especially in a no-service, or low-service, high flying economy, believe me it is important. If you lose focus of your customers your competitors may have a surprise waiting for you. Customer service is still important and alive today. Be sure you keep this fundamental fact visible and living in your business.

Mission Statements

I like to see small business owners have a mission statement. Unfortunately many don't but if they do the owner is the only one who knows where it is or what it says. A mission statement is of absolutely no benefit to the business if it is not visible and living within the organization.

When I worked for a large corporation we saw the mission statement in print in the employee handbook. It was interesting, I guess, but I personally never embraced it as I never felt I was in it. What I mean is that I was never engaged in the development or the conversation about the meaning and intent of it. Consequently I had no ownership of it.

On the other hand, a mission statement in a small company developed with the employees has a chance of being meaningful if they are included in its development and implementation. Visibility and ownership is critical if you expect a mission statement to be meaningful and not just a bunch of words that "they" made up. The statement should accurately reflect why the business is in existence.

I witnessed real employee ownership of a mission statement with one of my clients when the staff was asked to develop it. Imagine the empowering feeling for the staff when the owner asked them to develop the mission statement! And imagine the pride the owner had in observing this discussion!

Getting the Right People

What is possible in small businesses is only limited by the people within the organization. I endorse the words of Jim Collins in his book *Good to Great*, when he referred to the great companies they researched: they first got the right people on the bus (and the wrong people off) and then got them in the right seats *before* they decided where the bus was going. I talk about human resources in more detail in Chapter 8, Staffing the small business.

> **Fire yourself today, and ask if you would rehire yourself to lead the company to the next level of growth.**

Fire yourself today, and ask if you would rehire yourself to lead the company to the next level of growth. It must start with you. If not, get the right person to take and implement your ideas, or reconfigure them so you can expedite them and grow the company. You cannot tolerate mediocrity and substandard performance and poor attitudes in your company. Few companies that do will ever reach their potential and most fail.

I once heard someone say, "Not all plumbers are good businessmen and not all businessmen are good plumbers." How true! Be clear what you and your employees are capable of and are not capable of. Surround yourself with the right people and make sure they have the right seat. Too often people are in a position they either are not competent for or don't like to do but feel obligated to do it. If this describes you, change it. Don't wait for someone else to.

Empowerment

Several of my clients, once we have had a few days together, will confide in me some of their innermost fears and concerns. The fear of failure, without exception, is one of them. Yet failing at some things gives you the opportunity to learn and grow. Fear is at the root of their resistance to give up authority and power to employees. Once they start to give up responsibility to others, however, they will tell you the flood gates open.

It goes without saying you don't just throw authority and responsibility to people you don't trust, respect, are not competent, and are reckless in their actions. But rather, you allow people who show signs of responsibility and trust to accept more responsibility. With few exceptions, employees that are empowered will always rise to the occasion and more often than not exceed your expectations.

The same principle applies to you, the owner and manager of a small business. Out of stressful chaos you can create sustainable growth with clarity of purpose and a calm and committed focus you never had before. Again, if you have a clear vision of your existing company and you can see what is working and what the causes of constant frustration are, you can take action that can show you new opportunities. I don't suggest for a minute that you completely eliminate what you are doing. I do, however, strongly suggest that you examine what is going on, keep and leverage the good things, and eliminate the things that are counter-productive to your goals.

As a small business owner and manager it is so easy to get caught up in day-to-day operations that you start to micro-manage everything. You may actually think that you are the only person that could ever do the job(s) right. Wrong. I have observed that when small business owners and managers show signs of being good leaders, rather than "bosses", they start to break the fatal chain of control. When this happens, their businesses start to take off.

One of my clients is the perfect example. This client is engaged in the tree service business. His role as owner often conflicts with his desire to be an arborist trainer. His realization of empowering his staff has allowed him to excel at both. He leaves his business now for several weeks at a time to pursue his ambition to be one of the best arborist trainers in the world, while maintaining a business that is viable and supports him in his training role. How did this happen? He simply started letting go of the reins. He empowered some key employees. He made sure they were technically competent and then let them grow as individuals.

Recently he reported to me that they exceeded his production expectations by 14% while he was away on a training venture. Jokingly, I suggested he go away more often! But, it truly has opened his eyes to the power of letting people grow and certainly confirmed every word ever written on this topic. Empowerment is not about abandoning responsibility. It is about trust. Trust that every one of your staff can create greater value in the business.

Almost all of the businesses I work with as a consultant can raise the financial resources to grow their businesses, or have already done so. All want to grow to be multimillion dollar organizations and all of them have or will. Why? Because they were able to start putting business discipline into their lives and instill it in others. The power of having business discipline cannot be underestimated.

Overwhelming the Small Business Owner

Every small business owner has felt overwhelmed. Interestingly, all of my clients have expressed at one point or another that they too have felt overwhelmed while dealing with the daily machinations of their businesses. Overwhelm is the state, or mood, we get into when tasks and concerns pile up more quickly than our ability to deal with them, and we begin to feel weighed down with the excess. It actually feels heavy in your chest and can sometimes make it hard to breathe. Worse yet, there is no apparent end in sight.

Most people, when they hear it the first time, don't believe or want to accept the following notion: it is absolutely unacceptable for owners, managers, and leaders to allow themselves to be overwhelmed for extended periods of time.

> … it is absolutely unacceptable for owners, managers, and leaders to allow themselves to be overwhelmed for extended periods of time.

Of course, as human beings we are in and out of many moods everyday. The issue around this particular mood is that it is debilitating and destructive. As leaders we must recognize it as such. The key to living in and out of this mood is that you as owner, manager, or leader have considerable, if not total, control over the things that put you into this mood in your daily work life.

Early on in my consulting business I had a client come to me for help. I realized immediately that he was not expecting someone to run his business, but rather to help with the tremendous feeling of being overwhelmed he was experiencing day-to-day. When I told him he was the only person in his business that could do something about that feeling, I thought I might lose him as a client. He clearly did not believe he was in control of this situation.

He worked for many years in his business with the belief that if he didn't handle the "important stuff" it wouldn't get done. This is not uncommon among entrepreneurs. After many lengthy discussions he began to see that he, in fact, was in control of his feeling overwhelmed.

I looked at what his stated goals were and then looked at his schedule. Something didn't match. He was taking on too much, most of which he could have easily delegated. Once he began to see this it occurred to him that just on the other side of this feeling of overwhelm was opportunity. Slowly, as he got out from under the oppressive weight of this feeling, things started to open up for him that he never thought existed. Of course, this type of transformation does not happen overnight. It takes a lot of hard work and dedication. Fortunately the rewards are very much worth the effort. This client no longer feels overwhelmed in his business and he thanks me nearly every day for it.

Again, we are all human and do slip in and out of many moods, including overwhelm. The reason this mood is not acceptable for leaders is that it is the one mood we have a great deal of control over. Owners and managers are usually the only ones with the authority to eliminate, prioritize, or delegate the things that are causing these feelings.

When we as managers and leaders let the stress from day-to-day work show up to others who rely on us for guidance and coaching, we lose the ability to lead effectively. So how do we manage this destructive mood? The answer is in our ability to recognize that we are in this state and be even more resolved to do what it takes to get out of it as quickly as possible. This sounds easy, but some days it takes great will, effort, and determination to not let this terrible debilitating mood ruin your life

Being resolved and committed to eliminating the things that put you in this mood is not only possible but can lead to powerful results. By sitting quietly by yourself and writing down all the things you think are causing this repeated stress you start the process of physically removing the weight that you feel. Share the list with someone you trust and see if they see the same issues as you. Then start to eliminate things off the list, park things that you can't do anything about immediately, list things you need to start delegating, and be resolved to prioritize and do the things that are most important.

Remember, you are the only one that has the power to do something about this mood. Recognize this and be resolved to reduce to a minimum the effect it is having on your life and the life of others around you. You and only you are accountable to take charge before it consumes you.

Negative People

If you or your friends live in negative moods and dwell on the negative aspects of life, you need to seek some help to recognize what this is doing to your life. Likewise, if you have employees that dwell in the negative most of the time you need to either help them see a more positive outlook or get people who can see the positive. Nothing is more contagious than people feeding on each others' negativity.

While I won't pretend to be an expert in this field I can tell you that negative people in your life and business will have a tremendous drag on your ability to grow as a person and as an enterprise. The productivity losses alone are staggering and should make any owner want to jump into action to eliminate the cause or causes of negative influences in the business.

I have seen, and I'm sure you have too, the impact that constant negativity has on the people involved in it. You absolutely must not tolerate it in your business if you intend to have sustainable growth. There are plenty of resources available on this topic. If negativity exists in your organization do yourself a favour and act now to work toward eliminating the effects of it.

Invariably there is at least one person in each of my clients' organizations who spends the majority of their time in a negative mood. Having a consultant like me come into the company to talk about business discipline and offer tools for growth usually makes this person even more negative. I often get a comment like this, 'What could you possibly know that could help us?" After everyone else in the room picks their jaws up off the floor I propose that we get back to that question later. That person then stews for awhile longer.

Interestingly, it's not me, nor the rest of that person's colleagues, who brings him or her out of the negative mood. The negative mood starts to change when he or she sees that I am there to help the business, and by doing so I help each person *in* the business. On occasion this process takes several days, and more often than not that person begins to change their mood. The ripple effect of this change is felt by the rest of the team almost immediately and things really begin to happen. It used to surprise me that one person's mood could have such a big impact on a small business, but not anymore.

CHAPTER 2

A conversation with yourself

Are you mentally ready to take your business to the next level? Are you ready for the commitment that it takes to be truly successful in your business? This chapter will help you determine the answers to these questions. It will allow you an opportunity to check-in with yourself and determine if you are in the right place in your life and your business before attempting to take it to the next level.

More often than not, we go through several career paths in our working life. Once thought to be a sign of instability, holding numerous jobs in a number of companies is thought of today as a great career enhancement. The multitude of experiences enriches the scope and depth of a person to the extent that employers demand in today's market.

Too many people tend to lose their desire to learn early in their careers. The result is that they tend to have the same one year experiences over and over again, really getting nowhere. People like this do not easily learn new skills or optimize opportunities. Many would say they are stuck in the mud. Change from the norm in their life is seen as threatening and unnecessary. On the other hand, many that embrace the concept of continuous learning and change are rewarded with never ending opportunities and enrichment.

Small businesses employ the entire spectrum of individuals, from high school dropouts to MBAs. More importantly small businesses have people who want to grow their skills, character, and entrepreneurial skills. Many employees of small business see themselves as employees today and business owners tomorrow. Given the right environment in the business people can grow and achieve their personal goals and dreams.

Getting Ready to Grow

If you are in a small business today, it is likely you worked for others in one or more businesses long enough to determine that you were ready to go it on your own. This takes some a few short months and for others this occurs over a period of many years. Whatever the process that brought you to the point of truly engaging your entrepreneurial spirit, you're here and ready to go to the next level.

Getting to the next level in any business is a challenge. Key considerations in getting ready to grow include knowing that:

1. You are ready to take your business to the next level,

2. You have the right team in place,

3. You have the fundamental business components in place,

4. You have clarity about your goals

Take inventory of your values

Be clear about what you stand for and what your beliefs are. People will follow you when they are clear about what you are up to and where you are going. If you are clear on your beliefs and people see that you act according to those beliefs, they will be encouraged to follow your lead. Nothing is more discouraging to employees and peers than to listen to someone say one thing and do something entirely opposite. Impeccable character is a key factor to building and retaining trust.

Someone with a nurturing and encouraging mindset often develops a culture of trust for other employees. Everyone in your presence enjoys your joyful, yet committed demeanor. You have demonstrated to others your willingness to learn, listen with sincerity, and stay the course on your beliefs.

Honesty about your values can often be an eye opener. Check with someone you trust how you are doing. Ask them, "Do you think this is what I stand for?", or "Do you see my values this way?"

Without first being clear on your values, taking another step in growing your business can have risks. If your commitment to live by your values is unclear to you and people around you, success will likely be elusive.

> **If your commitment to live by your values is unclear to you and people around you, success will likely be elusive.**

Your personal values and the values within your organization must be aligned. It is difficult, if not impossible, to have double-standards when it comes to values. Your personal values are critical in preparing you for the personal and business decisions that will have to be made in the present and in the future.

There is a clear link between personal values and the trust and commitment you can expect from those close to you. If there is a consistent and clear demonstration of your values, others see that you can be relied upon and therefore trusted. Principled leadership will be tested and only the committed will prevail and be noticed. The old saying, "Practice what you preach", is a challenge, especially when things don't always go the way you think they should.

Be observant of others that are consistent in their values and beliefs. They are the true leaders and often carry themselves in a humble, yet charismatic way that others want to emulate.

Adopting someone else's value system does not work. It eventually shows up for what it is—a copy. Be true to yourself and those you desire to lead by being yourself and being authentic about what you say and how you say it. Simple truths and standards that are practiced and observable by others will establish a greater value system for the team.

Your credibility is yours and yours alone. No one can give you that credibility, it must be earned. By establishing a link between your values and your actions, your credibility grows and sustains itself. An inventory of your values periodically can establish visibility and an awareness that is needed to check how you are doing with your personal values. Again, your personal values are the foundation that your business values are based on.

To get started in establishing your personal values, you need to make visible your thoughts. You can start the process by taking an inventory of what you stand for. Ask yourself:

- What do I really care deeply about?

- Who are the most important people in my life?

- What do I have boundless energy to do?

- What things do I totally detest?
- What kind of people do I like to associate with?
- What do I do for others that I am proud of?
- What are ongoing dissatisfactions?
- What are the things that give me joy and pleasure?
- What am I afraid of?
- Do I have courage to challenge the status quo?

One of the most powerful gifts a friend, family member, or mentor can give to you is honest feedback. Talk to a trusted friend about your values. Through these conversations clarity about who you are and what you truly stand for will be forthcoming. This clarity will help guide you in your future endeavors. Examining your values is powerful medicine if you are not afraid of what you will find. List your values below.

My values are:

_____
_____
_____
_____
_____
_____
_____
_____
_____
_____

Success means different things to different people

Success is more than dollars. We tend to get caught up in the day-to-day rat race of making a living and accumulating financial assets. Some of these assets we convince ourselves we really need are really just "toys". I for one like having toys. But don't let the excesses drive and define your life.

We tend to put a lot of emphasis on the material things in life but at the end of the day you and you alone need to ask if that is what your life is all about. I do not pretend to be the guru of life skills. At best I can only hope to help you assess what is important in your life and what is less important.

We do put a lot of demands on ourselves and thus a lot of pressure and stress. How you prioritize these demands is your business. I can only tell you that I have a new interpretation of what is important in my life. I ask myself: If that thing was gone instantly would I really miss it, or be emotionally distraught about it?

Circumstances can change and so can what's important

Six years ago my wife Eileen and I decided to retire. We realized we would have to change our lives a bit and adjust to the new reality. One of the new realities was that in order to live full-time in our fifth-wheel trailer we would have to sell our home and put our lifetime of accumulated "stuff" in storage. We thought this would be for a few short years and then we would move back into a house, start mowing lawns, fixing, and painting again. The new reality is that we love the new freedom and lifestyle so much we want to continue it for the foreseeable future.

Over time all the "stuff" that we thought was so valuable when it went into storage turned out not to be. In fact it has become a liability. Not only don't we miss it, we barely know or care what all is in there.

The point here is that your circumstances may change and what you thought was of great value may in fact not be so valuable in the future. Be prepared to accept this, as it will happen to all of us in one form or another.

So what is valuable to me? That's easy—my family, my health, and my treasured network of friends. Fortunately, I always surrounded myself with people I respected and many I knew to be smarter than me. Invariably, I was successful in many endeavors because of what others helped me accomplish. I didn't know that to hire someone more skillful than me was supposed to be a threat, I just did it. And I was never disappointed. Over the years these people, who I knew were bright and intelligent, went on to much higher levels of accomplishment than I could provide for them. It makes me very proud to have been part of their lives and I feel humbled with the thought that I may have influenced them to become successful in even a small way.

What does success mean to you?

Success at home means:

_____

_____

Success at work means:

Now, write your success statement.

I will know I am successful when:

You should now have a clearer picture of what you stand for and whether the business growth compliments your personal values and success criteria. If they are aligned you are likely in a good place in your life to take on new challenges and growth.

CHAPTER 3

Deciding to grow

Many small business owners are in a constant state of decision-making regarding growth. It is, however, better to make conscious and deliberate decisions rather than have haphazard and unplanned growth that often leads to feelings of overwhelm and confusion. There are many ways to approach the challenges of growing your business and depending on your industry you can invent a strategy that works best for your circumstances.

Whatever your strategy, it needs to fit your values and fulfill your personal and financial goals. Further, it needs to engage your heart. You must believe that the motivating factors are truly what you believe and have a great deal of energy about. In other words, you need to have the personal strength and will to see the growth commitment through to success. Half commitments or part-time efforts likely won't produce a satisfactory or sustainable result. In fact, it can be personally debilitating and frustrating when your heart is not in it.

In most cases, when the business is established, there is a plan on paper or in the mind of the entrepreneur of where they want this business to go in the future. Inflexible plans seldom come to fruition and undisciplined plans seldom create long term sustainable value. Many books have been written giving advice on how to develop business plans. You may have read and indeed developed a business plan for your current enterprise. This book, as you have probably guessed, is not about business plans.

Whether you own a small painting business, run a manufacturing facility, or manage an oil field servicing business, growing your business with a committed discipline is a challenge. Your business may have grown in spite of any conscious efforts or planned action. Many small businesses grow because of the connections and networking of the owner and key employees. Others grow because they are a source of convenient products and services in a niche industry. Yet, in many enterprises there is potential for growth that has not yet manifested.

> **One of the most difficult things in any business is to have a clear and visible picture, or view, of where the business is today.**

One of the most difficult things in any business is to have a clear and visible picture, or view, of where the business is today. The challenge then is to have clarity about what the business will look like during and after disciplined growth.

There are many ways to visualize and document a business. Too often however, boxes, charts, and lines attempt to show the organizational structure and inner workings of a company, without necessarily involving any discussions or conversations. These approaches have failed to provide us anything of value to examine. Further, they are typically very mechanical, rigid, and easily become bogged down in the minutia of workflow. As valuable as workflow is I have yet to see a traditional workflow diagram tell me what is really going on inside a business.

Before examining an alternative to traditional methodologies, you need to ask yourself: Do I want to grow my business and if so, how and to what extent? What are the parameters I want to set in designing future growth that I can physically and financially manage? How can I engage others, especially employees, to be as committed to growth as I am?

These questions can be overwhelming if we don't take a logical and disciplined approach to answering them. First, you need to determine if growing the business is the right thing to do. Ask yourself: What is driving the need to grow the business?

Many of the small business owners I work with are motivated by a sincere desire to:

1. Provide a reasonable income and standard of living for their family

2. Provide a critical volume of business to sustain key employees

3. Provide sufficient income for retirement through operating income and/or capital gain

Scatterbrained growth and all the ideas in the world, even very good ideas, are not likely to produce optimum business results unless you apply proper screening and business discipline to them. We have all seen the results of too many ideas without the proper planning and prioritization in place. Great ideas often do not materialize, or if they do, are a disappointment at the end of the day.

Most of my clients are ambitious and innovative. They often have more ideas than they can physically or financially focus on. By exposing them to prioritization options they do not lose sight of their core business or the new emerging opportunities. By applying proven performance criteria ideas quickly get prioritized, developed, or shelved. Many shelved ideas may still be very viable pursuits, but the timing is not quite right. I talk more about this in Chapter 7—Opportunity Assessment.

Once you have made an informed decision to build and grow your business the work begins. The first and foremost consideration must be getting the right people and getting them placed in the right roles to ensure success of the new venture. Often this is overlooked or put in a different order.

Many of us think we needed to get the business in order to get the right people. While this can be possible, by far the more sustainable approach is to have the right people doing the right things prior to taking the company to the next level. Without committed and competent people, especially people who can grow personally and lead others, this expanded enterprise could be a frustrating waste of your time and money.

The other consideration is, of course, having the working capital and operating finances in place to facilitate the ongoing needs of the business during its growth period. Often, the financial barriers are easier to overcome than the need for committed human resources. Every businessperson I know that is in the process of growing their business struggles to retain quality men and women with the leadership qualities that can accelerate their business. The investment in getting the right people to do the right things is critical and can determine to a large extent the future possibilities of any business.

> **The investment in getting the right people to do the right things is critical and can determine to a large extent the future possibilities of any business.**

Balance work and life

Never assume that you don't need a balance between your work and your personal life. A close examination of that balance may reveal a warning sign for you to reevaluate your business pursuits. Don't ignore that warning, but rather internalize what is evident and take action to rebalance and be grounded in your decision to pursue your ambitions to grow your business.

In my consulting business we recognize the need for business owners and managers to have a healthy life in order to be successful in their businesses. We believe this so strongly that we incorporate a team of experts in this field as business associates. I believe balanced lifestyle strategies result in better business success. Consistently take care of yourself, physically and mentally, and you will reap both business and health benefits for the long term.

CHAPTER 4

Your business assets

Before making any decision to grow your business, you will want to do a thorough inventory of your current assets and status. It is always useful to understand your current situation, make grounded assessments, and be brutally honest about the current status of your enterprise. Having a clear picture of the platform you wish to expand will be useful in determining a "reality" about what is possible. Dream big and be ready to stay steadfast on the path to realizing the dream. Your visible and obvious zeal to see this growth to a successful end will require courage and determination.

Business Value

There are three main values to be considered in determining the value of a company—financial, pragmatic, and symbolic. Financial value is often predominant as it determines the share price or a monetary price for the business. The other two values, however, should be looked at carefully as well because the future of an organization is determined by the innovation and learning within the company and the perceived image or brand. An appropriate balance of these three values will optimize the overall value to a shareholder and potential buyer of an organization.

> ... the future of an organization is determined by the innovation and learning within the company and the perceived image or brand.

Financial value is the standard and measurable value used when determining the success of a business. Often, this is the only value considered in determining a sale price or stock value. It is easier to determine and measure than the other types of value.

Overlooked and often misunderstood is the value attached to a learning or *pragmatic* organization. Any organization that is not pragmatic usually cannot sustain itself as competitors will find ways to outrun it with new ideas and technologies. Blindness to this value would have never allowed a company like Microsoft to grow.

The last value, *symbolic,* or goodwill, is often overstated and difficult to measure. Owners that have built a company from the ground up place more value on this than others are willing to pay for. This inflated value placed on a company is often the point where sale negotiations fail. Exceptions to this would be the values attached to branded and well known franchises where purchasers pay a significant premium just to own the brand name of the franchise. Large sums of money are spent on creating a company brand and symbolic value.

It is worthwhile having a conversation about these values when assessing or designing your company or enterprise. A further challenge is to apply a monetary value to the pragmatic and symbolic values. What assessments can you make about these values in your company? Try to determine the financial, pragmatic, and symbolic value of your organization below. Consider what percentage you would assign each value of your business.

Financial

_____
_____
_____
_____

Pragmatic

_____
_____
_____
_____

Symbolic

_____
_____
_____
_____

Making assessments that are useful and reliable

Making assessments that are meaningful and useful requires discipline. First, let's look at what I mean by an assessment. An assessment is a statement that may be true or untrue—it is only an assessment. What makes it useful, and at times powerful, is how well it is grounded in observable action. The better the assessment is grounded the more useful it becomes. Ungrounded assessments can often be of no value and are equivalent to rumors, which are ungrounded assessments by nature.

Grounding assessments is what makes them useful. By grounding you want to use observable things that are as current as possible. The better grounded the assessment is, the more it becomes like an assertion, or fact. Becoming disciplined in making well-grounded assessments can help you with your day-to-day business decisions as well as other aspects of your life.

Negative assessments

Negative assessments can be extremely devastating to individuals or they can be a wonderful gift. A damaging negative assessment is one that is given in a mean-spirited rage to another person. A gift is a negative assessment that is well grounded and a great deal of caring and love is connected to delivering it. In order for a caring negative assessment to be given to another person, the giver needs to take great care to first get permission from that person to give it to them. Often when people are not in the right mood or circumstances the best intended negative assessment is neither heard nor received by the recipient.

All negative assessments given with permission and in a caring and loving spirit must only be given for the sake of helping the person or situation or for improving on a situation. Giving negative assessments for the sake of anything else can be devastating and harmful to the other individual.

Here is an example of a negative assessment: "Your performance in the last month of the year has not been up to standard." This assessment by itself is not particularly useful to the person receiving it. However, it does become useful and helpful to the person when it is grounded with current facts. For example, if the assessment was accompanied with detailed factual statements about what drove the assessment in the first place.

A better way to give this assessment would be to say, "Bill, I would like to give you an assessment about your performance in the last month. Would you be open to this?" If Bill is, for whatever reason, not open to this assessment then determine a time that would work for both of you to discuss this. If on the other hand Bill says, "Sure, what is it?", then you are all right to give the assessment.

This conversation might go as follows: "Bill, your performance this past month has not been up to the standard we usually see from you. Here are a few things I have observed that have caused me to bring this to your attention:

1. The construction materials list you forwarded to me yesterday was missing several key items and as a result will slow the crew down.

2. Two days ago you were late for a pre-job meeting that the crews expected you to be at."

Now Bill has actionable items to focus on. Without the grounding statements he would have to try to guess at what drove the assessment in the first place.

When is it appropriate to give well-grounded negative assessments? They are useful for:

1. Helping a person improve on a poor performance issue

2. Avoiding a situation that is producing poor quality work

3. Making better business decisions

We make negative grounded assessments for the sake of improvement and helping others. Permission must be obtained from the recipient to ensure engagement and open listening. Assessments that are not grounded in current observations are not particularly useful or reliable.

Assessments that are not grounded in current observations are not particularly useful or reliable.

A number of my clients have become quite open and honest about the use of assessments. Over time they have become very good at making both positive and negative assessments. They tell me that the caring use of negative assessments have helped them deal with issues that were show-stoppers in the past. Issues that got in the way of employee and business development can now be dealt with and action taken for the sake of moving their businesses ahead.

Now that we have looked at what assessments are, it's time for you to make some grounded assessments about the state of your business.

Assess your financial assets

As a business owner or manager of a small business you must have a good sense about the financial status of your business. With a big-picture perspective, take a look at the physical assets you have in place now. List the obvious big ticket items you currently have, such as trucks, equipment, office facilities, etc. and assign a current market value that you think they are worth if you had to sell them tomorrow. Then list what your debts are for mortgages, rent, and cost of goods. You will have in front of you what you normally carry around in your head about the status of your business.

If your business practices allow it, compare this list to the real financial status of the business as outlined on your balance sheet. If the written picture that you pulled out of your head looks anything like reality, it is likely you have a good handle on where the financial status of your business is.

Let me tell you about a former business partner of mine who knew where his business was financially on a day-to-day basis. He was a person I learned a great deal from as he knew the financial status of every one of his seven businesses at any given time. I was always amazed at how he did this with all of his companies.

While I was scrambling around to get the papers to show him the details, he had already calculated the current financial status of the company in his head based on the conversation we had on how many field crews were working and a few other facts. I always admired that and decided that I would strive to be more like him. As a result, I was more aware and conscious every day as to the status of our financial health and I paid particular attention to the roles of the people who influenced the finances the most.

This same partner came into my office about one year after we started up our business and announced he had "made it". When I looked at him I said, "Made what?" He replied, "I am a net millionaire today". This bright, yet unassuming individual, who started out as a teacher in Saskatchewan, six years later declared he was a millionaire. I always appreciated his influence and the impact he had on my life. Not as a millionaire, but as a focused and determined businessman that gave me a chance to be his partner and to learn from him. He is truly a cheetah in the business world.

Focus and Determination

Like my business partner, you will need to be focused and determined to be successful in your business. You need to be more involved and conscious about the financial status of your company without burying and paralyzing yourself in the details. So, how can you do that? Today it is much easier to do than it was in the 1970's and 1980's. You don't need to have a photographic memory or be a brilliant accountant. All you have to do is have some financial business discipline. You will note I talk a lot about discipline. I don't mean discipline in the sense of marching to a beating drum—I mean the common sense of paying attention to what is really important and making it a routine to know the financial health of your business.

My business partner used to tell me to let the small stuff go and focus on the big stuff. How true that was. You too can be better off to focus on the bigger picture and leave the details to others who may be much more qualified to do them. Your time is valuable in building your company and leading it to its full potential.

In the beginning, owner-operators and managers of small companies need to multi-task, however as you prepare for growth you will need to focus your energy and time on guiding the ship, rather than rowing in the hole. Again, if you have a good mental idea and picture of your financial status, and this picture is confirmed with financial statements, then you likely have all you need to start to move to the next level in your business.

If your financial results are not satisfactory, it may raise a flag for you to seek some professional financial advice. Your accountant is a good place to start. I highly recommend that you find a friend or someone you trust that is a successful business person to help you. People that have successful businesses can often look at your financial situation and offer good advice whether they know anything about your industry or not.

> **I highly recommend having an advisory board, made up of several business people, who would be willing to mentor your business through the growing years.**

I highly recommend having an advisory board, made up of several business people, who would be willing to mentor your business through the growing years. They do not need to be expert in your business as their role is to challenge what you are doing from an unbiased point of view. Often they see things that you and others in the industry would not.

Once you have an overview of your company's physical assets and liabilities you need to take a look at the equally important assets in your business: your employees and subordinates. If you have been in business for more than a few months, you likely know that you would not be in business without good people beside you.

When you look at who is in your existing business with you, ask the question: If I fired all of us (including myself) would I rehire us? If the answer is unequivocally yes, then you are likely in reasonable shape to start the process of growing your business. If not, you may have a significant problem to contend with. Like Jim Collins says in his book *Good to Great*, "You have to have the right people in the right seats", before you start the bus!

Assessing your human resource assets

Jim Collins goes on to say that you need to get the right people before you decide what it is you want to be "great" at. Interestingly, most of us did not follow his advice nor did we have the benefit of his research. However, I fully endorse this principle and see its tremendous value.

Assessing yourself and your current employees needs to be done with an open mind. Not so much trying to second guess what you may need and trying to fit people into those needs, but rather an honest assessment about the skill sets you already have in one form or another. Not all business disciplines require that everyone be at a high level of competence, however there are some that may be mandatory.

In the technical domain, you and your staff may have all of the right technical requirements you need. However, there are many other business needs and domains that will make the difference as to whether your company excels or ultimately fails. Assume you have people with the technical skills you need, but they do not possess good communications skills. In this situation you risk losing customers. What if part of the requirement for your crew leaders is the ability to write detailed reports and your current employees cannot? Soon customers will begin to become dissatisfied and you may lose them altogether.

If your employees lack negotiating skills they may be abrupt when things don't go as planned, thus causing upset customers and potentially other problems for you as expectations continue to be unmet. Perhaps most importantly, what if your key staff does not possess the leadership skills that you require in order to move the business to a new and higher level? Leadership skill can be the determining factor of success or failure of a business. It's clear that having your human resource assets in order is as important as having your financial business in order.

If you are making honest assessments about the current status of your business, from a financial and human resource perspective, you are one step closer to understanding what it takes to make the next step in achieving your business potential. The skills that you'll need to move your business forward are the subject of Chapter 5.

CHAPTER 5

Skills for growing and getting over the wall

Almost all small businesses hit the wall at one time or another in their evolution. While there are numerous tools and processes you may consider during your deliberations when you hit the wall, I will address a few that have proven to be tremendously useful to so many of my small business clients. Honest self-assessments in the following domains help form the foundation for growth and their application can help you get over the wall, or through it:

1. Negotiation

2. Leaderment

3. Leading Teams

Competent people make your business better however you cannot be blinded by competence when the right people are doing the wrong things. Part of your role as owner or manager is to continue to develop your employees' skills, and make sure they are applying those skills in the most beneficial way. The implementation of the three skills noted above is critical to any pragmatic organization. These organizations believe in continuous learning and I believe this is fundamental to business growth.

1. Negotiation

While negotiation is a topic of much complexity and study, I include here a brief review of some of the mechanics of this subject for no other reason than to give you an awareness of the topic and the knowledge that there are many resources to assist you should you want to explore further.

Negotiation is by definition a compromise between two sides. This does not mean you compromise your integrity, but that you are willing to give a bit on your position so that the issue can be resolved. If both parties enter into these conversations with their minds made up as to the outcome then a compromise or movement is unlikely. In this situation a win-win result is not usually possible. There are legitimate reasons why a strategy may be used to produce a win-lose or even a lose-lose result, however, in most negotiations we are clearly looking for a win-win result.

It is noteworthy that creating a win-win result is more likely to happen on a regular basis when the two parties have earned a mutual trust. Often when the trust weakens, the win-win begins to turn into a win-lose situation.

> … a win-win result is more likely to happen on a regular basis when the two parties have earned a mutual trust.

In my experience and training, any negotiation needs to be conducted in a calm and collected manner. This will allow for reason and common sense to nurture the conversations between the two parties. Often, elevated emotions will reduce progress in negotiations to a yelling match, and as we all know that never produces the desired results. My advice is to enter and exit all negotiations in a calm and collected way.

Learning to negotiate

Negotiation is a key ingredient in solving the day-to-day issues you face on the job. How you manage negotiations and conflict depends on your knowledge of the various styles used in dealing with conflict and having the skills needed to handle the strategies employed by others. The more we understand some of the basic skills and techniques, the more likely both parties will have a more positive experience. Let's examine some of the issues involved in negotiations.

Dealing with feelings

First, you must acknowledge that everyone has the right to their own feelings and that we must respect that right. This is not something that is necessarily natural to all of us or the people we have to interface with in our business life.

Determine goals and relationship

I must reiterate the need to secure a balance between the need to satisfy a goal, task or issue, and maintain a manageable personal and working relationship. I have often said I didn't need to love everyone at work, but I certainly had to respect the fact that we needed to work in a professional and business-like manner together. Your sincere desire to create a win-win result needs to be seen by the other party. They need to see that you have a sincere desire and are willing to look for mutually satisfactory solutions.

Choose a strategy

Each of us has a preferred style of dealing with conflict and that style generally determines our strategy.

There are typically five styles of conflict management:

a. **Avoidance**: Hide your needs or feelings from others and/or change the subject.

    Consequences: Negative assessments of self and others; issues remain unresolved; trust and respect are undermined.

b. **Accommodation**: Agree; "go along"; speak softly; use plenty of qualifiers.

    Consequences: Lower self esteem; negative assessments of others; goals may not be achieved.

c. **Compromise**: Reveal surface needs but conceal your underlying needs, use "negotiation talk" i.e. let's split the difference or "can we make a deal?"

    Consequences: Harmonious interpersonal environment; real issues often remain unresolved; price paid by compromise can lead to resentment.

d. **Competition**: Accuse, label, or blame others; use words like "should", "must", or "you"; nonverbally invade space.

   Consequences: Defend or counter attack; compliance generally accompanied by a desire to "get even"; trust and respect are undermined.

e. **Collaboration**: Openly reveal relevant needs; separate the people from the problem; listen; identify underlying interest.

   Consequences: Positive self-assessment and assessment of others; issues get resolved in a manner that allows both to win; trust and respect are preserved and the relationship is enhanced.

In order to manage any conflict productively you need to know what each style looks like and the outcomes it produces. Each style requires the knowledge of how to do it, when it would be appropriate to use, consequences of using it, and how to make it harder for others to use a counter-productive style. The skills that follow are needed to correctly choose the right strategy in a given situation.

Active Listening

Active listening means communicating that you are listening by displaying nonverbal attentiveness, perception checking, and paraphrasing. If you are thinking about what you are going to say next you run the risk of missing the other person's complete conversation and meaning. This will often lead to misunderstanding or result in the other person having to repeat what they said, proving you weren't listening to them. How often does this happen in your day-to-day work or personal life? How often does this happen when talking to customers? It's probably more prevalent than you think.

Communicate that you are listening to them by using your non-verbal communication skills such as: nodding your head yes, leaning forward and acknowledging that you heard them, and paraphrasing what you heard.

Assertion

Knowing when and how to be assertive without being offensive is a skill. Often it is appropriate to be assertive to clarify non-facts, make a factual statement or make well grounded assessments. You can often take their position and dramatize the implications. For example you could say, "If we take that approach we run the risk of being electrocuted". Or perhaps you could say, "If we do what you are suggesting we could lose many of our customers".

Confrontation

There is a real skill involved with knowing when and how to confront the person or problem without shutting down progress toward a positive outcome. It is important to know how to keep the conversation on a more steady level when emotions start to arise. Any confrontation is risky, but you must always enter and exit the conversation in a calm and relaxed manner. Both confrontation and assertion must be used with care and skill.

Creative Problem Solving

The ability to creatively solve problems can be demonstrated in a number of ways, including being able to: identify key issues, clarify stakeholders, increase trust levels, gain commitment, achieve quality decisions, and value cooperative involvement.

Try rating yourself using the following statements regarding negotiation:

- I usually use only one of these styles of conflict management
- I know when to use a different style to achieve the desired outcome
- I consistently use the collaborative style for all issues
- I can teach others how to use each style and when it is appropriate to do so

Training in negotiation is incredibly valuable and applies to all areas of your business, particularly in sales and customer service. An investment in negotiation skills training is exactly that—an investment, and should not be considered an expense. Whether we know it or not, or admit it or not, we are negotiating all day, every day of our lives. Your business can only benefit from skill development in this area.

All of my clients use negotiating skills. They tell me that just having an awareness of the skills necessary to negotiate win-win situations has been helpful to them. One client told me that he had never considered pricing a job for a customer to be a form of negotiating until the training he received at our seminar. In fact, most customer interactions involve negotiating and therefore require some level of negotiating skills.

2. Leaderment

A manager can be appointed, however it implies that the manager is a leader as well, which may not always be the case. Leaderment—a term I use to encompass many facets of management and leadership—therefore is the ability to be a manager by appointment *and* to exhibit leadership skills and influence. In other words, leaderment is a blending of management and leadership skills. Be clear that there are two distinct skill sets.

For now, I want you to consider that growing your company can and will be a real challenge and you need to possess leadership skills as well as the title of owner or manager. In a booming economy you may achieve growth simply by managing, but when the economy turns, or competition intensifies, leadership skills become increasingly important. Growth without leadership is attainable, but not usually sustainable.

> **Growth without leadership is attainable, but not usually sustainable.**

I believe to one extent or another we all possess some leadership and management skills. However, we often don't consciously take an inventory of how we are doing on a regular basis. Many people go through their careers thinking they were good leaders or good managers without being clear on what that really means. I will attempt to shed some light on, and provide some clarity to, this rather large topic in this chapter.

Leaderment is like the four legs of a chair: management is two of the legs and leadership is the other two. A strong and stable chair requires all four legs. Likewise we need to develop our skills in both management and leadership to ensure we provide a strong foundation for the company to grow and become stable.

Let's take a closer look at leaderment. It embodies the role of a manager and a leader and requires that you have skills and traits that will make others in your organization follow you and support your goals. In order for them to do this you have to display through your actions what you stand for, what you believe in, what you want to accomplish, and what it looks like when you are successful at achieving your goals.

Leaderment is about helping people achieve common goals and not about your position in the organization. While you may have a title, the power and influence you exhibit is driven by their belief that you say what you mean and mean what you say—essentially, you practice what you preach. And given your position as manager or owner, you are respectful and supportive of other people who are there to help you achieve your goals. Their input and efforts are appreciated and acknowledged to the extent that they feel valued. Another way of looking at leaderment is to say that you cannot simply declare that you are a leader—this is something that must be earned.

Traditional definitions of a manager include such statements as: can hire and fire; can implement policy; can discipline; can direct the work. The traditional terms that often describe leaders are: someone who believes "we" is more powerful that "I"; is innovative; supports creativity; embraces change by stepping out of the box; can inspire others to achieve; and allows others to take the credit. Here is a description of a person who displays leaderment at its best:

- Has authority by virtue of their position *and* has the respect of others at all levels for their observed quality of performance

- Assigns work to others while continuously seeking opportunities to support them and ensure their success

- May be a liaison between hierarchical levels in a company yet respects everyone as a fellow employee

- Rewards the efforts of others while inspiring them to achieve more

- Believes empowerment is the real driving force within the company

- Is the first person to help remove barriers for others

- Is open to challenging and being challenged for the sake of improvement

- Motivates and improves morale by exemplifying positive energy

- Seeks win-win in negotiations

- Has earned trust

Leaderment is required to fully develop and implement the Diamond Solution, which I will discuss in more detail in Chapter 6. By using the Diamond Solution, clarity can be achieved as to what is going on in your business as well as what is possible in the future. Your leaderment skills and abilities will determine the sustainability and effectiveness of its implementation. As you develop leaderment skills you will begin to see the positive results in your business that you were hoping for.

An example of the development of leaderment skills with one of my clients took place with a young man who spent the first 15 years of his work life driving a truck. He had decided that truck driving was no longer a challenge and he wanted something different. I had an opportunity to consult within this business and coach this young man for several years.

After a number of conversations together he saw that while learning the technical end of the business was necessary it would be his understanding of the business side that would determine his future. Over time he was offered an opportunity to learn a new trade and was promised that if he learned the trade and the business skills necessary he could own the business. I worked with him through the steep learning curves in management AND leadership skills. That young man today owns 100% of a thriving business that continues to grow.

A common theme that arose during my many interviews with industry leaders on this topic was that most companies do not spend enough time and money providing leadership training to their employees. The comments I received were, almost unanimously, that people are promoted with minimal formal training, and it often leads to less than expected results. Most often these skills are learned from a boss or over time and as one advances in their career they simply practice what their boss or bosses did.

That boss may be a very competent leader or may be incompetent. I had two superiors tell me, after I left a large corporation, that they were not good leaders. However, because of their *appointed role* in senior management, they tried to show up as leaders. In the several years I worked with these two they did not display the traits and qualities of great leaders.

Both individuals were highly competent in their chosen profession and were obviously promoted based on that fact. However, the promotions lead them both into a world where leadership skills were as important as their technical ability.

This did not make them bad individuals by any means, however, it made them poor leaders and therefore they were never able to motivate, appreciate, create, or make positive change in the organization. Simply, they were not effective in their roles in senior management. I was always appreciative of the bravery it took for them to tell me of their own inner fears and for that I applaud them both.

I have read that leaders are not born, but created—hence leadership has been the subject of a great deal of research and study. Hundreds of books have been written on leadership. My job in this book is not to re-invent the wheel in this regard, but instead summarize some of the key points on the subject, ones I feel are important for you to consider.

You likely have some management and leadership skills already. As you read this section, try to take an inventory and make assessments about your level of competence in this area. Remember, you can learn to be a better leader. Read about leadership, ground yourself in the fundamental traits of leadership and by all means follow and seek the mentorship of great leaders.

I recently spoke with a young man that was very proficient in is job as an arborist. He had achieved many credentials and was performing work as a crew member on a tree climbing crew. Throughout the conversation he was telling me that he was happy at his work and enjoyed his job and the other people on the crew. He was telling me that people would often come to him for help and advice. They would bring him ideas that they could work on together to improve their results and he would often see some of this innovation implemented in other operations of the company.

When I told this young man that he had just described someone that exhibits leadership traits and skills, he questioned it. Although seemingly quite content to be a regular fellow on a tree crew, he was describing some very strong leadership traits. I am sure before that conversation he had never thought of himself as a leader. I am also sure he pondered our conversation for some time into the future. This conversation simply re-enforces the fact that you do not have to be a manager to be a leader. We all know people like this young man.

For an incredible example of what leaders are and how they work I highly recommend the work of James Kouzes, chairman emeritus of the Tom Peters Company, and Barry Posner, Dean of the Leavy School of Business, and their book, *The Leadership Challenge*. Their work is recommended by many other leadership experts, including John C. Maxwell, who has authored many fine leadership books himself.

In *The Leadership Challenge*, Kouzes and Posner speak of the Five Practices of Exemplary Leadership. Their five practices include: Model the Way, Inspire a Shared Vision, Challenge the Process, Enable Others to Act, and Encourage the Heart. What do these words mean to you? Can you see them in your mind? Can you see the results you would obtain by manifesting these practices? I can, and it affects my thoughts and actions every day. These practices are critical to the success of any leader and my personal experience tells me that there are elements of each practice that we must exemplify every day to be successful. *The*

Leadership Challenge is perhaps the most comprehensive and inspiring book of its type produced in the past ten years. Get it. Read it. Live it.

Jim Collins is another great author that we can all learn from. In his book, *Good to Great,* he proposes that some of the great leaders of all time exhibited personal humility and professional will, and that is how they set their companies apart from the good companies. He also talks about the sustainability of the great companies being directly tied to the sustainability of their leaders to be great leaders.

Interestingly, a common trait of the leaders of what he and his team describe as the great companies were that people were promoted from within, not parachuted in from outside the company. While some for the really good companies did bring in celebrity and high profile leaders, the great companies had people from within their organizations take over their senior leadership.

If you are at all inspired to become a better leader I also suggest you read the many works of John C. Maxwell. He writes, "Leadership develops daily, not in a day". While leadership comes in a variety of styles and definitions there are common threads that exist when you see a true leader. Here are a few:

- Competence

- Trust

- Sincerity

- Empowerment

- Innovation

- Risk taking

- Celebration of success

Take a minute and complete a self-assessment on how you are advancing in the discipline of leadership.

_____
_____
_____
_____
_____

_____

_____

_____

Leadership skills and traits are not the only requirements, but can play a key part in your career development and business success. Further, whether you are in management, own the company, or are a new employee, you can learn new skills or improve your existing skills. For those of you that have had the opportunity to use these skills every day, I challenge you to be a mentor and help others develop and grow.

Continue Learning

Leadership can be learned. I liked the leadership comparison that was given to me by a good friend, Larry Abernathy, a Vice President at Davey Tree Expert Company—a world leader in the tree service industry. He said that the skills required to be a successful leader in business are very similar to the skills you need to be an Eagle Scout. Think about that for a minute. This implies that you are learning to be a leader at a very young age. Further, the younger you learn the skills, the more opportunity you have to grow your own competence and the competence of others around you.

If you look at a list of the skills to be a business leader, then at a list to be an Eagle Scout, they are strikingly similar. Larry pointed out to me that he clearly started his leadership training through this scouting organization. He recalls conversations while he was a scout about competence, trust, sincerity, empowerment, innovation, risk taking, and celebration of success. Leadership can be learned, and there is nothing more fulfilling than having others see you as a leader, regardless of your title or position.

3. Leading Teams

Leaders and managers, or those in a position of leaderment, often need to involve others to accomplish goals or complete tasks. As a small business owner or manager, your time is valuable. It's likely that you attend a lot of meetings in the span of a year and it is more likely that you find yourself needing the team to get things done. Often this involves gathering information and collectively coming to some consensus about what action needs to be taken. I can think of situations within some of my clients businesses where the owner will get the team together and seek some agreement on what needs to be done to take care of some ongoing safety hazard, or some wasteful practice that causes employees to be frustrated.

Team dynamics are a large factor in a growing organization and can affect employee moods and the performance of the whole business. Managing team dynamics is both an art and a science. Those that are good at it are quickly recognized and often are asked to lead teams. In some cases these skills are the reasons for being promoted to a higher level within the company. Leadership, leaderment, and the skills to lead teams are very much intertwined. In the following section I will attempt to make a few distinctions about leading teams that may be helpful in growing your competency to lead. I have chosen the work of Heller and Hindle, authors of the *Essential Managers Manual*, to give structure to this concept of leading teams.

First of all, as a team leader you have to have some leaderment skills—you need to manage and lead. The manager in you must coordinate, measure, and drive the team's efforts. The leader in you must guide people, listen, observe, and resolve conflicts. In other words you need to be sincere about making your team members feel valued. "Team" has nothing to do with spreading the workload, but rather pooling the collective skills and knowledge to achieve a common goal. The team leader needs to make sure that the entire team understands its purpose and goals and also understands the financial and time constraints under which the team will work.

The team leader is often required to keep the team on track by revisiting the team's purpose and goals. It is important that the team members are committed to put the team's goal ahead of their personal goals. Members need to understand and respect the individual roles on the team and be tolerant of others mistakes.

Any team will benefit from decisions being made on facts and not on emotions. The team leader can play a significant role in holding the members to a high standard of conduct and professionalism.

An important element of a team leader's role is laying out the ground rules as to how decisions will be made. For example, once the team has formulated a conclusion to a topic or issue, will the team vote on it? Will the team leader make the final decision? Or will the proposed solution be taken to an outside person to make the decision? The team leader can avoid a lot of bad feelings by clarifying how the decisions will be made up front at the beginning of the team's formation.

A very important part of the leader's role is to build trust and rapport with the other team members. If you want members to open up and contribute to the team goals you need to encourage them to openly discuss their ideas. This cannot be done when team members are distracted by overpowering individuals or constantly interrupted. Dealing with disruptive people in a timely and caring way will set the tone for team dynamics and, ultimately, the outcome.

> **Dealing with disruptive people in a timely and caring way will set the tone for team dynamics and, ultimately, the outcome.**

Keep looking for opportunities to remind team members of the power of a collective resolution, or outcome. As leader, you must always look for opportunities to praise those who contribute in a positive and constructive manner. Everyone's contribution has to be acknowledged and of value.

If a "show-stopper" problem confronts the team it must be dealt with swiftly and decisively. The leader needs to get the show-stopper out of the way as quickly and credibly as possible. Here are some suggestions on how to do that:

- Revisit team purpose and goal

- Commit to an immediate resolution to the conflict or "park-it" if appropriate

- Request outside assessments of the situation and possibly engage a facilitator

- Try to create an incentive to resolve the issue

If a person on the team is overpowering the conversation inappropriately, the team leader must take steps to deal with the disruption. These situations do occur and cause bad moods and lack of participation from other team members. It is not acceptable to allow this type of situation to continue.

A leader can take steps to resolve this situation by talking directly to the individual and having them see what kind of moods and disruption they are causing; coaching the individual to share "air time" and being considerate of others opinions; and, in extreme cases, asking the member to step off of the team.

When you are acting as a team leader you must never forget that team means "we". Never should "I" be in this conversation. The team produces the results, not the individual. Without the team, and the team recognition, members will not feel appreciated. Always give the team credit for outcomes. A pat on the back or formal recognition by a superior is often all that is required.

Leading teams is a valuable skill in any organization. Larger companies may have a great deal of discipline and formal processes to follow and other companies may not. Whether large or small the power of "team" cannot be underestimated, and you as the leader can make all the difference in the world as to the effectiveness of, and motivation within, a team.

The productivity of a well-lead and well-run team is significant compared to a random assembly of people who are unfocused or unclear about what they are to achieve, and how to achieve it. Some of my clients are in very hazardous businesses and they simply cannot afford to be inefficient or have conflict on the team. The owners of these businesses have confirmed how important teamwork is in their day-to-day operations.

It is worthy of noting that almost anyone can lead a team. It is not necessarily the right of the boss, or manager. Developing leadership skills can be enhanced by leading teams and the owners and managers in small businesses should look for opportunities for some of their more junior employees to lead teams. If you are a strong team leader, mentor others as they learn these important skills.

These and other leaderment skills are required to ensure your future growth and sustainability. As I mentioned earlier, you already possess many of these skills, however continuous learning will always be of benefit to you and your business.

CHAPTER 6

The Diamond Solution

The Diamond Solution represents my interpretation of how people can work well together to produce satisfied customers and generate value for your company. It is all about visibility and accountability and it produces amazing results for businesses. It is essentially about the interaction between two individuals, making, managing, and keeping promises and commitments for the sake of taking action and producing a desired result.

In business we often take seemingly simple concepts and complicate them or struggle to find answers to that which seems rather apparent. Why do these things happen? More importantly, how can we avoid them? More specifically—to break it down to its barest form—how can we really *see* the interaction of two individuals as they communicate with each other in order to agree on what needs to be done, and then carry out the action in a timely manner to each other's satisfaction?

I have spent the greater part of my career analyzing human interaction in the workplace and my answer to this question is what I call the Diamond Solution. The Diamond Solution is nothing more than a way to look inside the many critical conversations that help to make your business what it is.

The word diamond is derived from Greek, meaning "invincible". It is something of tremendous value, and those of the highest quality are free of defects and provide perfect clarity. For our purposes, the Diamond Solution provides clarity into the *internal defects* in our companies. The work I do with the Diamond Solution is intended to help make your company more invincible.

Pure and nearly pure diamonds are colourless and transparent. Business processes that are seamless and transparent provide an unobstructed *View* (note that going forward I often use the word View as a verb, as in being able to see something, and as a noun, representing a map or diagram of the Diamond Solution) into how your business works, and enables conversations that define how it should work in the future. Many small businesses are like rough cut diamonds when they start. As the business matures, it cuts away at the rough gem, relentlessly trying to make it a pure and perfect diamond.

As you learn the principles of this work and the power to observe the world in a simple yet very comprehensive way, you and the people around you will begin to change the culture of how you interact with each other. You will see the rough cut stone turn into the sparkling gem you always knew it could be.

This disciplined human interaction has a smooth and comprehensive flow to it that produces amazing results. All participants have to do is learn the flow of this conversation and have the discipline to apply it over and over until it becomes common in the way you have conversations that you expect will produce value.

The Diamond Solution is a common sense concept that, when observed and used consistently, will give you a competitive edge in your business. The secret is having the discipline to constantly apply it and build it into your business culture. Business discipline from this point of view is, as I mentioned earlier, the interaction between two individuals, making, managing, and keeping promises and commitments for the sake of taking action and producing a desired result.

The Diamond Solution is about business process. I know what you're thinking—flow charts or boxes with connecting lines. That is most certainly not what I'm talking about. It is *not* a traditional flow chart, nor a traditional description of a business process. Instead, it is a promise, or concern, that is being taking care of, in conversation and commitment between two people. Note that I said *two* people. The significance of this becomes clearer as you realize that the Diamond Solution is about a culture of accountability; one person, not "them" or a "team", but one person, being accountable to produce some result for another person.

> … the Diamond Solution is about a culture of accountability; one person, not "them" or a "team", but one person, being accountable to produce some result for another person.

The Diamond Solution allows you to physically view a simple, or complex, promise or concern to be taken care of, so that each of the steps are visible and agreed upon by both parties. Then, as the action is in progress, clarity of what transactions are taking place to produce a defined result can be tracked. If there are any breakdowns in delivering a promise for example, it is easily visible to both parties what went wrong and it can then be corrected. As you become familiar with the Diamond Solution and become more competent in its use, you will begin to see its application to every facet of your business, and life.

You can view a simple exchange between two people, a high level picture of your entire business, or a frustrating breakdown that occurred. You can view what is taking place within a small crew or department, or within your entire company. In addition, you can view the conversation of what your future enterprise can look like.

By making the conversations visible, you have a road map in front of you of what is happening, what is working, and what is not working. Once it is visible, the ability to correct things that have gone awry or are not working well is relatively easy. The key is to have a clear view of what is going on in your organization.

This clear view offers you opportunities to improve and expand. The magic is that once visible, you and your staff can see what the right thing to do is in order to improve the situation. The Diamond Solution takes the hierarchy out of the company and replaces it with accountability.

Here's an example of what is possible. A small company that I worked with had five departments: administration, laboratory, engineering, marketing and sales, and shipping and receiving. It became clear to the new general manager that the flow of customer care was not efficient. In fact there were "stove-pipe" departments that were their own small companies within the company. Accountability throughout the organization was not clear. Things got done when they got done, often leaving the external customer confused as to the status of their projects and often very dissatisfied with the timeliness of the results.

It was not clear who owned the customer relationships, nor was it clear who the internal customers were. However, by working with the department managers and a few staff within the organization, collectively the company was able to see where efficiencies were possible, where customer care accountabilities lay and where dollars could be saved to be reinvested into growth.

The bottom-line savings generated from this new visibility was over $400,000. Note that I did not generate the savings—it was the collective effort of the staff that created the savings. All I did was coach them on how to view what was going on. They made the corrections and suggestions as to how to make it better. All of which was produced from within their own staff. The key to this was making what was going on in the company visible, and giving internal staff the opportunity to fix it themselves.

Producing a *View* of your business as it is today, and as you envision it in the future, is a powerful and meaningful way to get started in sustainable growth. Clarity into your company's existing situation is critical because today forms the foundation of your future. You want to be able to savour and retain the good things, eliminate the bad things, and create greater future value.

I chose diamonds to illustrate conversations between people because diamonds imply value and clarity—exactly what the Diamond Solution can provide for you once you are familiar with its use. The more competent you become in viewing what is going on and forecasting the future, the more you will see opportunities open up for you. Often very complex and confusing situations, when viewed through the Diamond Solution, will become clear and action can be taken quickly and decisively.

Let me state again what the Diamond Solution is *not*. It is not a series of boxes and lines with arrows showing a path of action, or workflow. It *is* a conversation of commitment(s) between two people that creates clarity and leads to action.

I recently worked with a company that had nine staff. Its employees consisted of several crews with various levels of competence in the arboriculture industry. Because much of the work that arborists do is on private property the company is especially concerned with quality work and public image.

I spent two two-day sessions working with this team over a period of six months. The owner initially expressed concerns over investing in equipment for growth, crew efficiency, and providing stability for his employees so he could retain them for the long term.

As we looked closely at the company we found that many of the fundamentals were already in place. Once the owner clearly saw what was working well, it began to positively influence his confidence about taking the company to the next level. This meant people would have to take on more responsibility and operations would have to be efficient to provide the quality and quantity of work to keep the company viable.

Through the use of the Diamond Solution the owner was able to view his existing company, crews were able to view what was going on in their individual crews, and the whole team was able to see what the next level of growth of the organization would look like. Once they had some clarity I felt the energy level go up and the commitment level go up at the same time. There is no magic here. The Diamond Solution allowed input from all stakeholders, and through this input, buy-in and commitment. With minimal understanding they were able to produce tremendous results.

I like to ensure that at least one person in any small business has the competence to lead conversations around the Diamond Solution because that is the way the investment in learning becomes sustainable. The more stakeholders that learn the Diamond Solution, and live in this culture of accountability, the more powerful the company will become.

> **The more stakeholders that learn the Diamond Solution, and live in this culture of accountability, the more powerful the company will become.**

Clients who have advanced their skills in the use of the Diamond Solution will tell you how their lives and businesses have changed for the better. All will tell you that they have fewer breakdowns and broken promises and have more clarity into what works, and why.

There are seven components to consider in a conversation between two people using the Diamond Solution:

1. The action, request, offer, promise, or concern
2. Who is requesting the action, the Requester
3. Who is performing the action, the Provider
4. The right people
5. Assess and Agree
6. Action or renegotiate
7. The Sparkle

Let's examine what conversations take place on each side of the diamond in more detail. Note that I use the terms action, request, offer, promise, and concern interchangeably. Depending on the context and use of the Diamond Solution these are all acceptable terms to use.

1. **Clarify the action, request, offer, promise or concern to be taken care of**—this is where both the person doing the asking (Requester) and the person that will be doing the action (Provider) agree upon what is expected to be done and by when. Both parties will agree on the entire interpretation of the action that is required to satisfy each other in this conversation. Clarification *may* result in a slightly different interpretation of what is required however it will be mutually agreed upon before the action is undertaken.

2. **The Requester**—this is the person who is asking someone else to perform some action for them. This person may be a friend, business associate, or colleague. By asking someone to do something this person has obligations to the provider to ensure they have authority, are competent, and know they have options in delivery of this request.

3. **The Provider**—this is the person that has been asked to do something by the Requester. This person is usually qualified to perform the action. The provider has obligations to ensure they are competent and have time to complete the action.

4. **The right people**—this side of the diamond identifies all of the people, or stakeholders, that may be involved in completing this action for the requester. Consideration for the competence of the people involved as well as their capacity to deliver is critical on this side of the diamond. All parties need to be committed to making sure they have asked the right people to be involved at this stage. The question must be asked: is this a reasonable thing to expect this person to do at this time and are there others that need to be a stakeholder in the conversation? Note that the provider may decline or re-negotiate. This is where you make assessments about having the right people on the bus in the right seats before any major commitments are made to fulfill this promise.

5. **Assess and Agree**—this side of the diamond represents an opportunity to make individual and mutual stakeholder assessments about the ability to

deliver what the requester is asking. It is also where the provider can seek clarity about what is to be done and if they have the support to get it done in a timely and quality manner. The provider may go back to the requester to clarify timing, reporting requirements, options for delivery of the action, and quality. It is acceptable to decline participation (which may have consequences), commit to it, or renegotiate. It is also critical at this stage that all commitments are managed appropriately by all concerned parties. It is this side of the diamond where the standards are clarified and detailed as well. If outside resources are going to be required, this is where the arrangements and negotiations take place.

6. **Action or renegotiate**—this side of the diamond is where we often excel. In other words, when asked to do something, most people jump right to doing it, and often we miss the opportunity to assess and agree. Therefore, in the action side of the diamond, the provider completes the action or task as understood during the conversation with the requester. During this action we may need to go back to the requester and renegotiate such things as timing, scope, and other elements. As with the previous stage it is critical that all stakeholders involved in the delivery of this promise are managing their commitments in a timely manner. At any time in the progress of delivery of the promise or action it appears there may be delays in the delivery it is incumbent on the provider to advise the requester of these delays. It should be common practice that the provider keep the requester updated on progress throughout the project. Unfortunately this is not common practice in our business culture today. Normally the requester is constantly asking how things are going and expressing concerns about not being informed.

7. **The Sparkle**—this is the final side of the diamond and end of this transaction and conversation between two people. The requester tells the provider that he or she is satisfied, or dissatisfied. Often the sparkle, or declaration of satisfaction, is missing and that usually results in some dissatisfaction on the part of one or both parties. The question here is: did the requester just pay the bill, or were they happy about paying the bill? It is on this side of the diamond that both parties will assess what they have learned throughout the delivery of this action or promise and leverage it in the future.

The Diamond Solution takes the form of the *View* on the next page, which describes what I have referred to above. Note that the View provides a place to note the name of the View, the Date, and the person who created it. There is also space for comments at the bottom, where learnings are captured for use in the future.

The Diamond Solution
A view of a conversation of action and accountability

VIEW NAME	DATE	BY
Example	July 23, 2004	Bill Smith

NOTE: EACH DIAMOND HAS A TIMELINE AND A VALUE

7 THE SPARKLE
The provider declares completion and requester declares satisfaction. Learnings are documented for future reference.

6 ACTION or RENEGOTIATE
The provider takes action to complete the promise. Renegotiation with requester regarding some of the details may be required.

2 REQUESTER
The person making the request.

3 PROVIDER
The person accountable.

1 ACTION
Describe the action, promise or concern that needs to be taken care of.

5 ASSESS & AGREE
The provider agrees to the requester's conditions of timing, budget, etc. and commits to complete action.

4 THE RIGHT PEOPLE
Is the requester qualified and do they have the authority?
Is the provider qualified (competent)? Identify others who need to be involved. Do they have the capacity?

COMMENTS

In any transaction between two people there is value created. In any diamond, therefore, there is value. As you map out these transactions in your business using the Diamond Solution, you will see that value. As you view more and more actions and processes you will gain further clarity into your business and its value. If every transaction, or diamond, has value then all transactions added together must equal the value of your business.

> **Each diamond represents a process involving time, and therefore money, the sum of which add up to total revenue and expense of the company.**

Each diamond represents a process involving time, and therefore money, the sum of which add up to total revenue and expense of the company. The diamonds provide a view into the transaction, each of which have a cost and timeline attached to them. The view of all of the diamonds within a company gives you a view of all of the processes within the company. In addition, you can view all of the interactions of external stakeholders the company is involved with.

It is my observation that in our traditional North American business culture most breakdowns occur on sides 1, 5, and 7 of the diamond. From my experience approximately 95% of breakdowns occur in one of these three areas. In our business culture we usually excel at the *doing*. We often don't focus our attention on the details, such as confirming exactly what needs to be done, by when, and for what purpose. Not having an actual purpose is the culprit of a surprising number of breakdowns. We tend to jump into action and do it, without giving consideration to the other parts of the conversation. It is these other parts that ultimately cause us our frustrations, breakdowns, and inefficiencies. When we take care of all sides of the diamond we start to see improvement in productivity and staff morale. It also creates a competitive edge as you cut waste and optimize your operations.

For example, if you view a conversation describing the reoccurring process of taking the garbage out every day, there is a time and cost involved. The sum of this time and cost would be the annual expense for garbage removal. I would call this a View of the process or action of garbage removal.

Having a Diamond Solution discipline within your organization will set it apart. The Diamond Solution clearly identifies what is working and what is not in any organization at any level. It makes opportunities visible and manageable.

Normally, based on conversations with management and staff, one can view the interactions taking place in the company and with its stakeholders, and visibility of the actions that should be taking place and are not (or missing), become visible. Also, actions that are not producing the expected results become visible and therefore they become fixable.

The Diamond Solution is a powerful tool to accelerate corporate value as it becomes part of the culture of the business. Further, it is a culture where management and employees break down the traditional bureaucracy and hierarchy. The boss can be the provider as often as an employee. The Diamond Solution takes the personalities and finger pointing out of breakdowns and opportunities and gives a clear view for appropriate action. More importantly, it is clear who is accountable for what.

The Diamond Solution is about making and managing commitments between people for the sake of taking appropriate action and producing results. And the bonus is that the organization can eliminate waste and increase profits while increasing customer and employee satisfaction. It applies to daily life and in small and large companies alike. Once an individual has become competent in its use and others see the value it adds a change begins.

Most organizations, whether they implement the Diamond Solution in a minimal way or totally embrace the concepts, change for the better and do it quickly. The more training people have with its use the more value it adds. My experience with the Diamond Solution tells me that it is difficult, if not impossible, to ignore or forget its basic concepts and principles once you have learned and applied them. Having implemented the Diamond Solution for many of my clients I have never seen a case where significant improvement did not occur.

Employees who have been involved in working with it become engaged in the company values and in creating the company's future. More often than not, the "fixing" of what is broken comes from organization's employees. Outsiders rarely have the expertise or knowledge of the individual roles within a company and therefore cannot have the insight that highly involved employees have. The Diamond Solution extracts the expertise of existing employees and management and allows the fix to occur. Fixes are developed *by* the company *for* the company.

One of my client companies found that the results of embracing the concepts of the Diamond Solution accelerated very difficult decisions regarding their future business. The owners of this company had struggled for several years as to why they were working harder, yet loosing financial and emotional ground.

The Diamond Solution clarified their present business reality and accelerated their ability to make the *right* business decisions. As a result, a poor working relationship was severed and an independent business direction was taken. The bottom line is that these small business owners have renewed direction and ambition. Further, they have grown the business and have an enormous opportunity to fulfill their personal dreams.

Over and over, those that have sought out knowledge of the process have improved their personal and business futures. It does not happen by chance! Only by embracing and working hard at living in a culture of accountability and action are significant benefits achievable.

The Diamond Solution is not a shopping list of things to do but rather a way of living and working together. A humble acknowledgment of the value of others to an organization is required to maximize the value a company and management team can gain.

One of the hazards of the process is that it may be embraced by employees and some management and not by all senior management or owners. My experience is that sustained and optimal results require that the top of the organization lead the transition to the Diamond Solution.

Example #1 of the Diamond Solution using a simple View

To illustrate how the diamond solution works, we will use a real life example of a simple transaction between two people to complete an action. Let's say that your supervisor makes a request of you to get some financial information together on a client's invoice payment history. Keep in mind that every side of the diamond must be completed carefully in order for it to sparkle.

1. Clarify the action—gather all pertinent financial information regarding the XYZ Company invoice payment history by 2:00 PM today so the Requester can be updated.

2. Requester—the supervisor of accounting, Sue.

3. Provider—you, Betty.

4. **The right people**—Your supervisor has made a request of you to get the information of payment history of the XYZ Company. Since your role at the company is in the accounts payable department, you have assessed that you are qualified and capable to perform this action. Sue has the authority to make this type of request of you to do this task.

After some thought you have determined that you will need to ask a peer employee for her assistance in procuring all of the information that has been requested. In discussing the needs with your peer, agreement has been reached that she can deliver in a timely manner the information required. Your personal assessment of this person's ability is that she will deliver the material on time as requested as she is consistently reliable.

5. **Assess and Agree**—You have determined that you can deliver on Sue's request for this information in a timely and efficient manner. You have clarified what is required and by when. You have committed that if it cannot be delivered on time as needed you will let her know in a timely manner with options as to when you can deliver on her request. At this stage both parties are clear on what is expected, who will deliver it, and by when.

6. **Action or renegotiate**—You and your colleague go about the task of gathering all of the pertinent financial information that is required. Files and information are gathered and packaged for delivery to Sue by the time promised. You have considered that if this could not happen by the time it was promised you would advise her immediately so as not to cause further breakdowns with the external customer that needs this information. Once completed you advise Sue that the information she requested is complete and on her desk.

7. **The Sparkle**—After you delivered the information to Sue she thanked you and your peer for the good job and for the timely delivery of the information. In other words she declared that she was satisfied with the effort you had put into keeping your promise to her in this matter. Sue will likely make future requests of you as you continue to prove yourself reliable.

Example #1

VIEW NAME	DATE	BY
Retrieve payment history	October 2, 2005	Scott Demo

6 ACTION or RENEGOTIATE

You physically go to the storage room and gather up the requested files and information. You take them to Sue's office and put them on her desk. You advise her you've completed the task.

7 THE SPARKLE

Sue acknowledges receipt of the files and information and tells you, "Thank you, good job." The diamond is complete.

2 REQUESTER

Accounts Payable Supervisor, Sue

3 PROVIDER

You, Betty

1 ACTION

Please provide me with the payment history of XYZ Company by 2 P.M today and put the file on my desk.

5 ASSESS & AGREE

You have assessed that you have the time and the ability to fulfill this request and can do it on the timeline requested. You assure Sue that if there are any delays anticipated you will advise her immediately.

4 THE RIGHT PEOPLE

Sue has the authority to ask this request of Betty and is competent in this domain. Betty is employed in Accounts Payable and has the experience and capacity to perform this task.

COMMENTS

This was a simple example of the Diamond Solution and a transaction between two people that worked and produced the desired results. All sides of the diamond were completed and thus the diamond sparkled because Sue was satisfied with the outcome.

Example #2 The Diamond Solution where things didn't work well

Now, let's look at a scenario where there was *no sparkle* and the promise was not met to the requester's satisfaction.

This scenario starts with one employee asking another to procure some ink cartridges for the printer as the ink has run out. The office administrator is aware that the field crew is out all day performing yard maintenance for customers around town. Today the administrator phones the crew and asks that they pick up a cartridge for the printer so she can continues producing client invoices and crew paychecks for payday.

The transaction is as follows:

1. **Clarify the action**—Pick up a printer cartridge from the drug store so I can do invoicing and payroll.

2. **Requester**—the administrator, Gene.

3. **Provider**—the assistant gardener on the crew, Phil.

4. **The right people**—the assistant gardener, Phil, is on the crew and decides he can do this action.

5. **Assess and Agree**—Phil mentions to the crew foreman to drop by a drug store on the way home and the foreman agrees.

6. **Action and renegotiate**—After the workday is over the crew stopped at the drug store and Phil went in to purchase a printer cartridge. He is pretty sure it is a z550 Cannon printer so he pays the $24.95 for the cartridge and goes back to the crew truck to go home. The next morning he stops into the office after their first job is completed to give the cartridge to Gene.

7. **The Sparkle**—Gene was busy so Phil just leaves the cartridge sitting on the counter and says goodbye to her for the day.

Example #2

VIEW NAME
Pick up printer cartridge

DATE
March 11, 2006

BY
Daryl Blair

7 THE SPARKLE
Gene arrived to work and noted the cartridge had been dropped off. However it was the wrong one; invoicing was behind; and it was payday, and she needed to print paychecks.
She was annoyed.

6 ACTION or RENEGOTIATE
Phil did stop off on the way home to pick up the cartridges for the z550 Canon printer he was pretty sure was at the office. The next morning he dropped the cartridge off to Gene.

2 REQUESTER
Administrator, Gene

3 PROVIDER
Assistant gardener, Phil

1 ACTION
Please pick up cartridge for the printer at work so I can finish the invoicing.

5 ASSESS & AGREE
Phil determined that it would be possible for him to complete this request with no other help. He could pick it up on his way home, then drop it off in the morning to Gene.

4 THE RIGHT PEOPLE
Gene has the authority to make this request.
Phil is capable and has the capacity to fulfill this request.

COMMENTS

On the surface this transaction appears to go relatively smoothly. However, it will serve to show all of the potential breakdowns that can and may happen in this scenario. Let's examine this closer.

After the administrator was finished what she was doing when the assistant gardener dropped of the cartridge, she went to the counter, picked up the package and went back to her desk. Upon arrival she pulled the cartridge out and discovered that it was the wrong cartridge for that printer. While there was a Cannon z550 printer in the office, she needed a cartridge for the one she uses for printing invoices and payroll checks. It was an HP4180.

She wasn't very happy about this waste of time as she had lots of work to do and invoicing was getting behind. She immediately got a hold of the crew foreman and explained that she needed the right cartridge immediately in order to get on with her job. The crew foreman saw it was important so went to pick up the right cartridge for her immediately. When he dropped it off the administrator thanked him for the quick delivery of the right cartridge.

If you can imagine this simple case study, you can see the waste that was produced by not getting the request clear in the first place. You will note that the burden of getting that clarity was on both the assistant gardener and the administrator. Further, the administrator never said when she needed the cartridge by, consequently got it the next day instead of the same day when she needed it. The assistant gardener should have asked when she needed it by.

Also, the administrator did not specify clearly the make and brand of the cartridge and as a result got the wrong one. This caused a double trip, lost crew time, fuel wastage, and frustration on everyone's part. Had the administrator been available to receive the cartridge the likelihood of her catching that it was the wrong one would have meant she could have fixed the problem more quickly.

These types of inefficiencies occur daily in every business in the world. The secret is to avoid as many of these breakdowns and inefficiencies as possible by gaining clarity and insight into what they are and taking steps to ensure they don't happen.

So what could have been done differently in this case?

The administrator should have asked for a specific cartridge to be picked up, and asked if it could be done by a specific time. Time is a critical factor missed in most transactions that I work with clients on. It's important to just stop for a moment and ask, "By when?" The administrator should have asked if the assistant gardener had time to pick up the cartridge and bring it to the office within the next 2 hours. If not then by when so she could have done other things without wondering when it was going to be delivered. Maybe it would have worked better for the crew if the foreman went to the drug store and on his way to lunch he could have dropped it off at the office.

Not getting clarity and agreeing right up front on what is required, by whom, and by when are the most common breakdowns I see. In Western culture we are generally good at performing tasks and completing actions but we are not particularly good at giving feedback when someone has completed a job for us. We don't always give or receive a declaration of satisfaction at the end of the job.

In many cases we do work for someone, send them an invoice, and they pay it. Do we know if the customer was satisfied, did the side of the diamond get cut perfectly, so it will sparkle? Customers often pay the invoice but we never really know if they were satisfied and would recommend you to their friends. Or were they just glad to get the job done and get you off their property and not likely call you back?

The Diamond Solution, if understood and followed, will produce a significant reduction in wasted time, frustration, and dramatically increase efficiency. In addition, it can give you a bird's eye view of larger issues. You can view a single operating crew, or you can view a much larger corporate structure.

Example #3 Inventing a new and expanded company using the Diamond Solution

Let's look at the small garden landscape company we just saw in the previous example from a high level structure point of view. In this case we will use the Diamond Solution to *view* the landscape gardening company we want in the future—where they have $2 Million in sales and several departments, with managers in each department. There is a small garden supply store that is an integral part of the future business. Because of the rapid growth in the area of the town they operate in the sales forecast is quite well within the realm of possibility. The owner now needs to get *clarity* on what he will need to have in place for this to be a successful enterprise.

Let's invent this company using the Diamond Solution.

1. **Clarify the action**—What promise or concern are we taking care of? Let's try something like the following. Keep in mind that this is all done in conversation, perhaps with other employees, friends, or business stakeholders.

    The promise might read something like this the following:

In the next two years build a sustainable landscape gardening company that includes field service crews and a garden shop that produces $2 Million in sales and profits for shareholders while ensuring staff is paid competitively, treated fairly, and feel respected, and where we collectively exceed customer's expectation 90 percent of the time.

That in a nutshell is the entire reason that this business exists. While the statement appears to be simple and perhaps may have missed a few things, the majority of why this business exists in encompassed by this statement. There is a specific financial goal, satisfied customers, profits for shareholders, and happy employees—an excellent description of the action or promise we are trying to keep.

Now, the action noted above may not be the perfect statement and may, over time, be enhanced and changed to better describe what this company is really up to and what it is not. Every Diamond Solution View, or map, that is produced to support this statement must align with its overall goal. I will show you shortly what I mean by that.

If anyone is doing anything within the company that does not directly or indirectly support the promise or requested action then you must ask the question, "why are we doing it?" This statement becomes the reason you are in business and the focal point of your collective efforts.

You can begin to see that a well thought out promise is worth the time and energy to ponder. It becomes the focal point of the business and it is absolutely critical that key stakeholders within the company see it, participate in the development of it, and embrace it. For if they don't it becomes like a worthless mission statement hanging up in the corporate hallway: useless and ineffective. It's not good enough for the president of the company alone to embrace the concepts within this statement but rather all employees.

The importance of this idea of employee support and buy-in cannot be emphasized enough. Companies have failed because the president did not have staff aligned with the principles and future direction of the company. Part of getting clarity of what your future company will look like must include, by design, key employees and stakeholders.

The next side of the diamond represents the *who*—the Requester and the Provider. Who is making the promise and who is delivering on the promise?

2. **Requester**—Nancy

3. **Provider**—Hugo

    Always avoid the situation where the *who* is one in the same person. This means that the person making the request for this action is the same one accountable for delivering the action. This rarely is a good thing, although it happens once in a while. If it is unclear who the requester and provider are, ask who will pay for this action or who the investor is.

    Other critical breakdowns occur when the person who has promised to deliver, the provider, is a group, or team, or multiple persons. It must always be an individual who holds responsibility for the promise. This does not mean that a team is not ultimately going to assist with the delivery but it does mean only one will be accountable.

    I've already mentioned that you should never make a promise of this nature and magnitude alone, so assuming this was developed by key stakeholders the promise should be made to an individual. For the sake of this illustration we'll say the promise is being made to the owner and sole shareholder, or president of this company. Then who is making this promise to deliver?

    What I highly recommend you consider is that the owner of the small business form a board of advisors that he or she trusts and knows to have business competence that can act on behalf of this company. By so empowering this board, paid or not, the owner is available now to be the promise holder and can focus on delivering the promise.

    Another alternative is for the next person in command to be the provider. Let's say there is an eight year employee that acts as manager when the owner is away for short periods of time. You can see that in a $2M company the roles of some key employees will likely change and now in this stage of the discussion the owner needs to assign the new required role. The second in command in the new company will be the general manager, or the owner's most loyal, trusted, and competent person and he or she will become the promise holder.

    Now we have a person that has a promise made to them, the requester, and someone who is willing to step up to the plate to take the actions needed to deliver on the promise, the provider.

4. **The right people**—This side of the diamond is all about competence and capacity requirements. In this case certain qualifications are required of

some of the staff in order to conduct this business. This is the time to ensure you have the right people and to clarify what your human resources will be. It is also a time to ask: Are the people I will be asking to help capable and do they have the time and capacity? If not, where will they come from and how will I ensure we have the right people?

The provider needs to have the authority to do what is necessary to get the right people to achieve the objective and deliver on the promise. This does not mean they get a blank cheque, it means that as requirements are met this person ensures that the plans are in place and financial resources are in place to bring on the right people.

5. **Assess and Agree**—Pay particular attention to this side of the diamond. This is the side that most often causes breakdowns due to lack of attention to detail. Most people simply don't take the time to assess the situation and have the appropriate discussions to determine the specifics of what is to be delivered. Instead of rushing off to do what we think needs to be done we should spend time up front considering:

- The resources you need to deliver the promise
- The timing—what needs to happen and by when?
- The quality and standards required for this to be considered successful
- The commitments you need from others before you can start to deliver the promise; for example external suppliers
- The measurements (for example, accounting and reporting)
- The deliverables; macro and micro-level
- The options: commit, counteroffer, commit to commit, or decline
- What stakeholder commitments you will need

Remember, by far the largest percentage (90% or better) of observed breakdowns could have been avoided by taking the time to flush out this side of the diamond. This area causes the greatest source of frustration when performance is not up to standard or expectation.

You can go back to renegotiate the central action or promise any time you feel you may not be able to keep the promise. There is a risk to this as time might be of the essence or commitments the company has made depend on timely delivery of the corporate promise.

However, it is acceptable to renegotiate if it is done in a timely and appropriate manner. For example, the two year timeline may not be realistic, so it is perfectly acceptable to negotiate a three year timeline. The owner, in this case, may agree that it is more likely to happen and is more comfortable with this approach. It is not acceptable to blindly accept the role of promise holder or provider and then fail to deliver results in a timely manner. If you hold the promise to deliver something to someone, you are obligated to keep the requester informed at all times.

Once all the considerations have been assessed and negotiated—for example what other promises and requests need to be made and to who and by when—in order to deliver this promise, then and only then can implementation and performance start. It is at this stage of polishing the diamond that you declare you are committed to perform and complete this promise or action. Now that you have assessed and agreed to the **what** and the **by when** you can go to the action side of the diamond.

6. **Action and renegotiate**—It is here where many, many new little diamonds appear. This is where the day-to-day activities are done. This is where each individual little diamond, or promise is made. The multitude of small diamonds can and should be segregated into the major promises or actions that have the largest value to the company. They represent the key functions and processes that are necessary for the delivery of the overall corporate action or promise. These include:

    - How the crews will work together
    - How the equipment is maintained
    - Who is accountable for customer contact and follow-up
    - How the store will operate
    - What are the safety standards and reporting relationships
    - How administration will operate and support the company
    - How the crew work is dispatched
    - Who does the equipment purchasing

The secret here is to address the big ticket items and not get buried in diamonds so you can't see the glitter. When working with clients I discuss, through conversation, the diamonds that are perceived to be the largest or most important.

Occasionally a small cost item is viewed as though it may have very significant impact on the image of the company. For example, we would create a diamond for how the crew appears to the public or how the storefront and grounds appear. Good judgment and sound assessments are made as to what is important and what is less important. In this case the public image of the company is important so we would pay particular attention to it.

All throughout the delivery of the promise or action checks and balances, assessments, and performance measurements need to take place. Often things don't go as planned. A new look at the situation in light of something unexpected is easy by using the Diamond Solution to examine and decide what needs to happen from there. Breakdowns are relatively easy to fix, once they are visible. The key is timely visibility.

7. **The Sparkle**—After the promise is delivered, the final step to complete the diamond is the declaration of satisfaction (or dissatisfaction). In the case of a corporate level view of this magnitude, in reality you would never go two or three years without several small-scale declarations over the time that the promise is being fulfilled. In other words, there would be frequent assessments about progress as the business grows and develops.

    The diamond is complete when the declaration of satisfaction is done, and there are numerous ways this declaration can be made. For example, the president may give performance bonuses to staff, or take everyone out for a celebration of success, and so on.

    It should be abundantly clear by now that the diamond will not sparkle if any side is not produced carefully. If any side is not polished with care and diligence, it will tarnish the clarity. Without clarity you will not have an unobstructed view into your business processes, and thus you cannot fix what you don't see.

Example #3

VIEW NAME: Grow landscape business
DATE: August 13, 2006
BY: Joanne Cameron

7 THE SPARKLE
Once the action and promise is delivered, the Requester declares satisfaction, all learnings or modified Diamond Solution views are documented so they can be revisited if certain breakdowns occur in the future.

6 ACTION or RENEGOTIATE
Once all the Diamonds have been well thought out in conversation, you begin the performance and action to deliver on the promise made. Renegotiation of some details may be necessary.

2 REQUESTER
Owner (or chairman of the board), Nancy

3 PROVIDER
General Manager, Hugo

1 ACTION
In the next two years grow a professional and sustainable landscape business with $2 million in sales that provides a safe, secure working environment for satisfied employees and that exceeds external customer expectations.

5 ASSESS & AGREE
There are numerous conversations to take place. Each and every one is a Diamond Solution View of its own. We usually only view key ones that are large-ticket-items or have a large impact on the enterprise. There is a requester and provider for each View.

4 THE RIGHT PEOPLE
Nancy has the authority. Hugo is capable and has the capacity.
Other stakeholders who need to be part of this conversation include other key employees, possible employment agency to attract key people, the financial institution dealt with to obtain loans, and other stakeholders.

COMMENTS

Summary of the Diamond Solution

The Diamond Solution is about making visible (a *View*) a promise between two people for the sake of taking action. It requires some training to become competent in its use and can be used at all levels of any organization. It is *not* charts, boxes, and lines of workflow within a company. At its core it's about conversations and its output will change the effeciency of your company.

The Diamond Solution can and has changed lives and companies. It reduces breakdowns, gives clarity as to what needs to be fixed, and shows you opportunities you never knew existed. It creates a culture of accountability and action. It enables you to see your future company and describes how it will work. And, as you become familiar with how it works, you'll never look back.

My clients who have used the Diamond Solution to examine their business processes repeatedly tell me that they cannot believe the clarity it has given them into what used to be a blurred list of things to fix. The real power, they say, is that the people involved in the day-to-day operations usually have the answers and that the Diamond Solution simply draws them out and adds order and visibility.

CHAPTER 7

Opportunity Assessment

We've seen how the Diamond Solution can help you see into your enterprise in a new way. It allows for opportunities to fix breakdowns and physically see what is happening during the most important interactions, or conversations, in your business. What it also uncovers is even more opportunity to expand and grow your business—organically and otherwise. What do I mean by organically? Essentially this means that the Diamond Solution identifies ways to improve upon the processes and resources that already exist. For example, a *View* (a map or diagram) may identify that Joe should be doing customer service instead of Fred. It may show that orders should be placed from head office on Tuesday mornings, not from the field office on Wednesday afternoons.

These discoveries all fall out of the views that you will create using the Diamond Solution. These are all organic and ongoing. You have not added capital or staff, or modified the overall business in any significant way. That is the beauty of the Diamond Solution—it does not require a massive overhaul of your organization.

But what would happen if the Diamond Solution uncovered something even greater? What would happen if it showed you that you could increase the value of your organization dramatically if you opened up a store in Dallas, or hired a new senior customer service person, or created a new product, or bought the assets of a competitor? Would you have the wherewithal to pursue one or more of these opportunities? How would you know which one, if any? How would you assess these opportunities? Would you go with your gut, or use some other method? That is the focus of this chapter.

Working with many small businesses as I do, I often have discussions with owners and managers about how to grow and when. These entrepreneurs often have dozens of ideas about new products, services, business lines, and companies. Those that have worked with the Diamond Solution also see options when they see inside their business and ultimately hold their bag of diamonds for the first time. "Neil", they begin, "what do you think of this idea?" Before I even have a chance to ponder the question they follow with an excited burst, "Or how about this one?" Vibrating with energy now, they continue, "You know, I've got about a dozen ideas I could work on, what do you think I should do?"

The reality is that my opinion, or assessment, under these circumstances doesn't really mean much. It's just an opinion, and everybody has one. Opinions are thrown around too often and too easily as though they are analogous to well-researched and scientific fact. In reality, they are not that at all. Now, I am more than happy to work with clients on rectifying issues brought forward by the Diamond Solution, or look at other entrepreneurial ventures, but one thing I won't give you is my opinion about what you should do—only you can answer that question. What I will do is ask you to work with available tools and methodologies to help you come to conclusions about what takes priority and what does not. This, too, is a business discipline, and is not always easy to do.

I can tell you first-hand that this discipline has saved several of my clients from potential financial ruin. What do I mean by discipline in this case? I'm talking about *Opportunity Assessment*, a method for scoring or prioritizing where your precious resources should be directed.

I'm sure it's happened to you several times, the question of whether to pursue opportunity A or B, or both. When the Diamond Solution brings into view C, D, E or any other number of opportunities you may begin to feel overwhelmed. As a small business, it is often not possible to pursue all of them, at least not all at the same time. The trap that many businesses fall into is trying to do everything at the same time, often spending considerable energy, and ultimately delivering nothing. Does this make them bad owners and managers? No, it just means they didn't have the tools to help them prioritize their opportunities.

The trap that many businesses fall into is trying to do everything at the same time, often spending considerable energy, and ultimately delivering nothing.

It may at first feel like you are abandoning something you feel strongly about but I prefer to call this *deferment*. You are simply deferring until the time is right or until it is determined that the opportunity is not worth the expense. Do you throw away these ideas or potential opportunities once you have decided to pursue something else? Absolutely not. You simply put them in a vault (more on this later), and stash the key somewhere safe. Again, you are not throwing anything out—you are just making the conscious choice to put it away until the time is right.

The 'right time' is influenced by many things, including market conditions, personal issues, finances, competitive forces, legislation, or lack of resources, to name a few. If you regard deferment as a failure or do not believe you can come back to the vault to retrieve your opportunities then you are sunk. On the contrary, you must view the vault as part of your intellectual property (IP), or capital. It belongs to you and your business, and hence goes with the business, wherever it goes. Without getting into IP law let's just say that there is value in capturing your ideas and prioritizing them for their present value. Do not throw anything out—you will regret it later.

So what is Opportunity Assessment anyway? At its core, Opportunity Assessment is about applying a meaningful scoring methodology to a series of criteria that relate to your business, and then prioritizing them based on their score. This prioritization determines which opportunities receive immediate attention and which go into the vault for future consideration.

Evaluation

Ultimately, ideas, concepts, processes, and other opportunities that fall out of the Diamond Solution need to be evaluated. Without evaluation, they are opinion, and opinion, as I have already mentioned, can lead you down a wrong and very expensive path. In order to evaluate these opportunities you need to develop a fundamental set of criteria against which they will all be evaluated. By developing these criteria, you will level the playing field such that all ideas or possible opportunities get a fair and unbiased shake. What this attempts to do is eliminate the 'pet project' from the list and exposes the truly powerful opportunities.

Must Meet vs. Should Meet

So, how do you develop a list of criteria? The first thing I do with my clients when developing this list is to determine what are absolute 'must meet' and what are 'should meet' criteria. By this I mean which criteria, or elements of an idea, product, or opportunity, is absolutely critical to the success of your business? These form the backbone of any and all opportunities that you may look at in the future. You should be able to say with confidence that if Opportunity X or Potential Product Y does not satisfy the must meet criteria then it simply cannot be pursued at this time. Let's not forget that simply having a great idea about a product or service will not guarantee that you will be successful in developing it. We're not there yet, though. We're trying to determine what even makes it to the next step. Put your foot down about these 'must meet' criteria. Here are some examples:

- Must have strategic alignment with overall business strategy
- Must satisfy all legal and legislative restrictions
- Must be technically feasible with current infrastructure
- Must have a payback period of three years or less
- Must have no 'showstopper' or killer variables at present time

There are potentially hundreds of must meet criteria for your business but best practices suggest using no more than six to eight. Any more than that and you may find that none of your opportunities are even going to get past the first step. This part of the process is more about *evaluation* than *elimination*. If your small business identified four potential new products and services after having worked through the Diamond Solution, would you automatically pursue all four? You won't know until you determine what criteria the new idea must meet in order to continue the evaluation.

'Should meet' criteria are those that are not 'musts' but form the basis for most of the evaluation. If your idea does not meet a particular 'should' criterion, it does not automatically take it out of the running as it would if the idea did not meet a 'must' criterion. If you have five or six must meet criteria you may have a dozen or more should meet criteria. These criteria are then grouped based on theme or common features. Here's an example of some general 'should meet' criteria that would require further specification depending on your business:

- Market attractiveness
  - Market size

- Market growth
- Competitive landscape
- Product advantage
  - Unique benefits
  - Value for money
  - Better meets customer needs
- Leverages company's core competencies
  - Marketing and sales
  - Technology
  - Operations
  - Industry and trade relationships
- Risk vs. Return
  - Return on investment
  - Rate of return
  - Low cost and fast to do
  - Certainty of profits/cost reductions
- Technical feasibility
  - Technology gap
  - Complexity
  - Technical uncertainty

Vault

I refer often in this chapter to what I call the *vault*. A vault can, and should, be a physical location that you put ideas that have not yet reached their opportune time. Whether it be a filing cabinet, a box, a folder on your computer, or a corner in your basement, the vault is critical to Opportunity Assessment. As I mentioned earlier, this is part of your company's intellectual property, and it is of value to the business in more ways than one. It's most critical application is in the evaluation of potential new ideas that benefit your business. The other application is in the intellectual property that exists within your business that somebody, someday, may end up purchasing.

Let's say you evaluated a product idea two years ago that just wasn't quite ready due to a new municipal by-law that would not allow it. Let's also say that you and your team spent several months developing the idea into a product that could be launched almost right away but the by-law stopped you cold. Let's also say that you threw out all of the documents, papers, spreadsheets, and other information that you had gathered on this idea because the new by-law made it impossible to launch your product. Now, two years later, there is a new municipal government in power and they have reversed that by-law. What would you do? You'd probably scramble to try to piece all of your old information back together. That is what a vault is for. I've seen clients put ideas away for years, waiting for the right time to bring them out. The vault is invaluable and should be used at all times. How many times have you heard the saying, there are no stupid ideas? Well, find a place to put them, all of them!

> **I've seen clients put ideas away for years, waiting for the right time to bring them out.**

Scoring

Must meet criteria are scored simply as Yes or No. Did your idea, concept, product, or opportunity meet the must criteria? It is either Yes, and continue on with the evaluation, or No, and put the idea in the vault. Should meet criteria, on the other hand, must be scored on an individual criterion basis, and then added together to determine the idea's overall merits. This is done by assigning a value of 1 to 10 for each criterion, with 10 being the highest, or most likely to succeed. This is all based on information available at the time of scoring. As more information becomes available the scoring may change, thus another good reason to keep previous ideas (and their scorecards) in the vault.

Typically, ideas are scored against each other, thus giving them context. For example, you may look at three seemingly similar ideas and your first reaction may be to do them all. But, after having scored them, you may determine that although all three met the must meet criteria, the scores in the should meet criteria were significantly different. The scoring, in fact, may have showed that Idea #2 was the clear winner and the others not really close. It is important to be brutally honest when scoring ideas. Artificially inflating the score on any one criterion or any one idea will not benefit anyone, especially your business.

An alternative to comparative scoring is to institute a minimum score cut off. That is to say, ideas that fail to reach an identified minimum score will not make it to the next step of evaluation. Of course that doesn't mean it should be thrown out altogether. It should go to the vault for potential future evaluation. The minimum cut off is typically used by companies with more experience using the scorecard, and thus have more data to determine what that minimum should be. This is more of a predictive model, whereby the company has sufficient data and experience to know that a certain minimum score is required to not only get to the next step in the evaluation, but perhaps the idea or product has a high likelihood of being commercially viable and successful.

> **If at all possible, depending on the size of your business, I suggest that you have more than one person do the scoring.**

If at all possible, depending on the size of your business, I suggest that you have more than one person do the scoring. That is to say, have multiple individuals do an entire evaluation separately from each other. The owner or owners plus any senior manager or managers should take the same scorecard and score the ideas independently. This further reduces the chances that the 'pet project' will slip onto the priority list. I have seen more than one occasion where partners in the business scored opportunities completely differently. Just having gone through the process they determined that taking no action was the best choice at that time. It may have cost them significant time, money, and headache, to pursue any of the ideas without a common understanding of the objectives.

Scorecard

Based on the criteria list provided earlier, the Must Meet section of the scorecard would be as follows:

Must Meet Criteria	YES	NO	Notes
Strategic Alignment			•
Legal and Legislative			•
Technical feasibility			•
Payback three years or less			•
No 'Showstoppers'			•

The Should Meet section of the scorecard would be:

Should Meet Criteria	SCORE (1-10)	Notes
Market Attractiveness (30)		
Market size		•
Market growth		•
Competitive landscape		•
Product Advantage (30)		
Unique benefits		•
Value for money		•
Better meets customer needs		•
Leverage Core Competencies (40)		
Marketing and sales		•
Technology		•
Operations		•
Industry and trade relationships		•
Risk vs. Return (40)		
Return on investment		•

Rate of return		•
Low cost and fast to do		•
Certainty of profits/cost reductions		•
Technical Feasibility (30)		
Technology gap		•
Complexity		•
Technical uncertainty		•
Total	**/170**	

Non-Action

It is important to note that at no time should your business pursue opportunities simply for the sake of it, or go after a 'cool' idea that has little or no value for the business. Even if the simultaneous scoring of several ideas indicates a clear 'winner' it does not mean that your business is necessarily ready to pursue it. The idea may have passed all of the criteria, and is clearly a better option than the other choices, but it still must be looked at in context. The context is going to differ greatly depending on the type of business you are in and many other individual factors that are specific to your case.

Non-action has been a powerful result for several of my clients as they work through Opportunity Assessment. One client of mine had many seemingly great ideas that he could have pursued and he was unsure which way to go. Dozens of ideas came to his mind as he considered the best ones to potentially pursue. After working through the scorecard it seemed that only three of these ideas had the potential to truly impact his business in a positive way. After looking at these three opportunities in context it was quite apparent that it simply did not make sense to sink any time or money into them at that time. They were seemingly sound concepts but upon further evaluation it was decided that non-action was the correct route at the time. This decision ended up being a valuable one indeed.

Process

At the very least, the process of evaluation through Opportunity Assessment will identify three key things for you and your business. First, it will engage you in determining what the 'must meet' criteria are—giving you a chance to look at the real critical success factors of your business and making you think more deeply about what evaluation truly means. Second, you will discover, or perhaps reinforce, some of the main criteria that you should be using to evaluate opportunities. It's possible that you may already have been using an evaluation or scoring methodology in the past but Opportunity Assessment brings it all into one place. Third, you will discover what ideas and concepts seem to apply best to your current business situation. As your business grows and develops the criteria may change also. The way a five-person company looks at a $50,000 opportunity is quite different than the way a 25-person company looks at the same opportunity.

Now what?

Let's assume that you have, over the course of several weeks or months implemented the Diamond Solution and identified a dozen potential new opportunities. You have also taken the time to score these opportunities using the Opportunity Assessment scorecard and determined that four of them clearly stand out from the others. Now what? Well, firstly you give thanks for the fact that you did not spend time investigating and pursuing twelve different ideas. You made the investment in the process and will now address only four ideas that seem to have some real potential. Now it's time to engage a development process to move your idea or product forward.

Before getting into the actual development however, it is important to get all your ducks in a row from a corporate point of view. You are currently sitting on four potentially solid product ideas based on the scoring methodology but you still have not made any commitments to their development. Who will decide whether or not to move forward? This is where stakeholders come into play. Stakeholders for your business could be any number of players: an investor, a wife or husband, the bank, a business partner, a senior manager, a board of advisors, and others. What part will they play, and why?

Before moving forward with your four ideas you need to set up a process whereby the appropriate stakeholders approve or disapprove of moving the project forward. Stakeholders are effectively what are called *Gatekeepers* in product development lingo. Gatekeepers are given the authority to say one of four things to your project as it moves forward through the various steps from idea to launch, again using standard product development terminology: 1) GO, 2) Kill, 3) Hold, or 4) Recycle/Redevelop. The first three are obvious, the last entails providing additional information or modifying the project in some way to meet pre-determined success criteria.

So, you have criteria, scorecards, and gatekeepers. Now you need to apply a development process that will take these solid ideas through to commercial products. This chapter is not about product development so I won't get into much detail but at the very least your process should include a number of steps after the initial scorecard, typically consisting of:

- Sizing or scoping
  - Research and investigation into the idea
  - Gather all available data and determine high-level parameters
- Business Case
  - Develop case for the idea, using everything you know about it up until that time
  - Include cost/benefit and financial projections
- Build product
  - Development of product based on agreed upon specifications
- Test product
  - Using beta (or initial) test group or market
  - Include feedback into re-build
- Launch product
  - Prepare for launch to market
  - Make available to target market and engage sales and marketing processes
- Post mortem
  - Review success based on goals and objectives
  - Usually twelve or more months after launch

The use of gatekeepers in this entire process is critical as they are required to give the project the go-ahead before each step. If they do not provide the go-ahead the idea/project should be put into the vault along with documentation explaining when and why it ended up there. If they do provide the go-ahead then the necessary resources should be available to engage the next step. The gatekeepers are essentially authorizing the use of the company's resources to move the project to the next step.

Summary

The Diamond Solution is a powerful tool for gaining insight into your business. It is also a powerful tool for uncovering opportunities that you never knew existed. Whether or not to pursue these opportunities is a critical question for most small businesses. If you decide to pursue an opportunity, how can you be sure it is the right one, and the right time? That is where Opportunity Assessment comes in. It provides a methodology for evaluating ideas based on Must Meet and Should Meet criteria. Scoring ideas against one another using the criteria and scorecard enable you to actually see how one opportunity stacks up against another. These tools are invaluable to small business entrepreneurs as they attempt to grow with limited resources and limitless imaginations.

CHAPTER 8

Staffing the small business

Many small business owners have a good product or service offering. With hard work they are able to establish successful, profitable operations. Only a few, however, are able to build the kind of business that continues to create new opportunities and adjusts to take advantage of those opportunities. Few break away from the many and become healthy, vibrant, growing businesses.

A relatively few high performing organizations are able to grow beyond the average company building a reputation for excellence and profitability to match. The successful ones, the highest performing organizations, have one thing in common: they recognize that breakout success demands excellence in three areas. The three pillars upon which companies are built are investors, customers, and staff. Breakout businesses strive for excellence and balance in all three areas.

Since the small business owner is often the primary investor, little needs to be said about the importance of caring for the interests of the investor(s). Likewise, little more needs to be said about the importance of customer service in building a breakout business. Though too often ignored, most business leaders have received endless advice on the essential nature of excellent customer service. On the other hand, most businesses need to hear more, and do more, about excellence in managing its human resource.

Most organizations espouse the old adage that a business' greatest assets are its employees. Breakout businesses modify the old adage and then implement it with consistency and diligence. First, they recognize that the employee is NOT their greatest asset. Their greatest asset is the RIGHT employee. Companies that come to grips with this principle commit to hiring, retaining, and motivating the right employees and quickly moving all others out in pursuit of what is right for them. If you want to build a breakout business, start by building the right team.

Building the Team: four basic steps

The four basic steps to building the staff you need to lead the growth of a breakout business are:

1. commit to investing in building the team ahead of growing the business
2. move the wrong people out
3. move the right people in
4. protect your assets

The Commitment

Too many companies place priority on finding new work to grow the business first, then they attempt to hire the team to complete the work. Then, when new business lands on their doorstep, they rush about looking for staff to do the work. Hiring decisions made when the pressures of a contract or looming new opportunity tend to give priority to expediency rather than excellence. Can a company be excellent if mediocre employees fill key positions? Of course not. If people of mediocre ability fill your key positions, your business is destined to be mediocre.

Breakout businesses commit to building a great team, and they keep building that team in advance of their growing business. It takes vision and it means investment. Perhaps that is why so few companies are breakout companies. If you have confidence in your product, then commit to building a great team. If you do it well you will be able to breakout from the pack, meeting and beating the competition. It is very unlikely that you will do so without the right people on your team.

Moving the wrong people out

Perhaps the only thing worse than not having the right people on the team is having the wrong people on it. Unfortunately, one of the most difficult things a business manager does is terminate people. Because of its perceived difficulty, termination of low performing employees or those with destructive attitudes; those that for whatever reason are not right for the future of the company, is delayed for months or even years. Too many managers choose years of stress, negativity, and low performance over 15 minutes of discomfort in a termination interview. Inaction affects the manager, the rest of the employees, and cannot help but affect the business. The manager should also realize that inaction affects the offending employee as well.

The manager who wants to build a breakout business must make sure the difficult decisions are made and implemented. A consistent and fair process that assures that the employee knows of the deficit and is given opportunity to correct the deficit is essential. That process, however, must not drag on indefinitely. The sooner one acts once it is decided that an employee is not right for the team, the better it is for everyone, including the terminated employee. Remember, not only is that employee not right for your team, but chances are the problems being encountered are a result of the fact that your team is not right for them. The short-term discomfort of the termination process creates for the former employee new opportunities for a better life. Most importantly, it creates a healthier environment for those that remain.

Moving the right people in

Almost every industry in North America is struggling with a dwindling supply of well-trained talent. Few think this is going to change any time soon. In fact, most think the trend will continue for the foreseeable future. These conditions make finding and retaining good employees a great challenge to the small business owner or manager. Many leaders bemoan the harsh reality of the labour market. Successful leaders that are looking to the future, however, accept it for what it is and formulate strategies to meet the challenge.

As previously mentioned, too many companies place priority on finding new work to grow the business first, then they attempt to hire the team to complete the work. As a result, businesses are prone to making two critical errors: 1) hiring the wrong person and, 2) overlooking the right person.

Decisions made in this environment more often than not result in hiring the wrong person, the average person, or worse yet, the below average person. Mediocre personnel do not staff breakout businesses. They staff mediocre businesses. Companies that have a strategy of always trying to catch up to opportunities by making do with whoever is readily available do not meet and beat the competition. Breakout companies take their time, hire with excellence in mind and they do so in advance of growth.

Of course, having the patience to search for the right employee does not mean you will find the perfect individual. We must accept the fact that there are no perfect employees. So, if you have to hire an imperfect employee, look for one with the right faults. Do this by thinking to the future. Hiring for the future requires finding people with leadership ability, vision, attitude, attention to detail, and other innate qualities upon which you can build your company. Be careful not to overlook great talent due to easily correctible deficits such as lack of experience or limited technical skills. The right people are your greatest asset so be willing to invest the time, and if necessary the resources, to build an excellent team.

Breakout businesses prepare for growth rather than react to it. They take their time. They hire the right people and they settle for nothing less.

Protecting you assets

You have done it right. You waited to find the right people, the people that are able to help your company reach your vision, outperform the competition and maximize your profits. It took time and it was expensive, but you have finally found the person or people that are going to make your early retirement a possibility. What is the biggest mistake you could make now? Remember, that person, the right person, is your biggest asset. The biggest mistake you could make now is to fail to protect your asset, to let that person leave; taking your investment and your future with them. Once you have hired the right people, you must be sure to retain them.

So, how do you retain key employees? The simple answer is, it depends. It depends on the employee. The 48-year old manager may be motivated by financial reward while the 35-year old supervisor needs respect and responsibility. The 32-year old foreman may want consistent hours, holidays with family, and long weekends while the 20-year old field technician will feel undervalued without access to the cell phone, notebook, and other gadgets with which he is so familiar. One of the hardest things for some business owners to realize is that it is unlikely that what motivates them will motivate those of other generations, gender, economic status, and so forth. The successful leader will realize she does not need to understand her workforce. She does, however, need to understand what drives them to come to work and be productive. The strategies used to retain and motivate need to be designed accordingly.

> **The successful leader will realize she does not need to understand her workforce. She does, however, need to understand what drives them to come to work ...**

One thing that does seem to be universal is the need to be valued. Valuing your staff means making them a partner with you. Not necessarily a financial partner, but a partner with a vested interest in the company's success. Communicate with them about the challenges faced. Solicit advice from them and take their advice seriously. Give them responsibility, the opportunity to succeed, and the opportunity to fail. Share with them the victories and let them see that your success means their success.

Staffing the Breakout Business

Many small businesses are one-person operations. Often this fulfills the financial and internal needs of the owner and is consistent with the vision for the future. Other small businesses have a different vision. Many owners envision a vibrant and growing business where several people are required in order to break away from the pack. They envision a business performing with excellence. As previously discussed in Chapter 6 everyone in this type of organization is a requester or provider on a daily basis. Your business is dependant on having people that are reliable, trustworthy, competent, and can function at a high level.

If your desire is to own or manage a breakout company, start by recognizing that the future success of the company is dependent upon those that manage, supervise, and perform the work. The company will do nothing without the staff. The company will not achieve excellence without excellent staff. Therefore, invest most of your energy and your resources into building and developing those that will either make or break your company.

Commit to building the best team. Hire the best. Get rid of the rest. Then fight hard to protect your asset and to help it succeed.

CHAPTER 9

Employee Involvement and the Value of Money

Not all employees will necessarily become owners. So how can you, the small business owner, help your employees and other key stakeholders gain their own financial security? The best advice I can give, regardless of strategy, is to start early. Employees with the majority of my clients often don't necessarily see what they, as individuals, gain from some of the business improvements that are being implemented. They can see the benefits for the owner, or owners, but not necessarily for themselves. If they are involved early in the process, and engaged on a financial level, they are more likely to stick around to the see the fruits of their labour.

When I consult with clients I introduce a conversation about employee involvement and their financial security. This involvement is a key example of developing and building trust with your employees. Start by exposing your employees to simple yet powerful financial tools early on and everyone involved will benefit. It is not necessary for you to be the financial advisor to your staff—in fact that is something you might want to avoid—but your support of their efforts to seek such advice is critical for building trust and involvement.

All of the small business owners I deal with value and care for their employees. A few have implemented innovative ideas to help their employees improve their financial status. Ideas range from starting up an investment company that employees can participate in to company share purchase plans. In all cases these employers are prepared to invest in the financial wellbeing of their employees. They believe it is good for the company to have employees concerned about their financial future. I couldn't agree more.

> **My advice to you is to encourage all of your staff and stakeholders to pay close attention to the value of their money.**

My advice to you is to encourage all of your staff and stakeholders to pay close attention to the value of their money. Share this chapter with them and help them see how money and wealth can accumulate over time. The below information is invaluable to all of us, regardless of age or circumstance. Seven of the most common sense fundamentals to the value of money are as follows:

1. Set aside 10% of what you earn *

2. The rule of 72

3. Time value of money

4. Relationship between the goose and the golden egg

5. Risk management

6. Diversification of investments

7. Home ownership

* Must become a habit. See definition of "habit" by Stephen Covey, below.

1. Set Aside 10% of what you earn (Obtaining seed money)

Set aside 10% of what you earn. It does not matter how much you earn. Whether it be $500 (teenager), $25,000-$75,000 (adult) or $1,000,000-$5,000,000 (company/business), make setting aside 10% a HABIT.

Stephen Covey says that a habit is a principle you internalize and has the elements of:

a. knowledge or "what to do" (set aside 10%)

b. skill or "how to do it" (put it into savings/money market account)

c. attitude or "why to do it" (do it without fail)

You will have a difficult time moving ahead financially as a company, an individual, or a group of individuals (family) if you do not have the 10% habit.

2. Rule of 72

This rule calculates how long it will take to double your money at a given interest rate compounded annually. To determine the number of years, divide 72 by the interest rate of your investment. For example,

a. at 3% it would double in 24 years (72÷3 = 24)

b. at 12% it would double in 6 years

c. at 20% it would double in 3.6 years

To understand the dramatic effect of this principle, consider investing $100 per month for 30 years.

a. At 3% you would have $58,300

b. At 12% you would have $349,500

c. At 20% you would have $2,298,000

3. Time Value of Money

Why is a dollar worth more today than 5 years from now? This erosion is due to inflation.

Example #1

If you lent $1,000 to a friend and assuming an inflation rate of 5% (the historical average), you would receive the following "real dollars" back depending upon how many years it took for the friend to pay you back:
After 5 years: $779
After 10 years: $607
After 20 years $369
After 30 years: $224

Example #2

Suppose you go to Tim Horton's 5 days a week and spend $2 each day. Let's say you decide to skip Tuesdays and Thursdays and save $4 per week ($16 per month) in the process. If you put your money into an investment returning 10% for 40 years you will end up with $101,000. With inflation eating into your savings at a rate of about 4%, the $101,000 in 2047 will be equivalent to about $32,000 in today's dollars, which would buy you a nice car upon retirement.

Should you want a fancier car, then only go to Tim Horton's on Tuesdays and Thursdays and invest $24 each month—you could then buy a $48,000 car.

4. Aesop's Fable of the Goose and the Golden Egg

Never confuse the principal (goose) with the earnings (golden eggs). The 10% you are setting aside each month is increasing the value of the goose. The investment earnings that you are getting from the goose are your golden eggs. If you kill the goose by spending the principal, you will not get any more golden eggs. You will be living perilously from day to day.

5. Risk Management

When we invest, we are at greater risk if we do not have an "exit strategy". If you are going to invest $5,000 in IBM, for example, you should at the same time decide how much you are willing to lose in the event the stock should go down before liquidating the investment (usually 10 to 15%). This way, you will have most of your principal to invest in something else or in the same company if it "turns around" and still has sound fundamentals.

During the technology bubble of the late 1990's and early 2000's, many people converted several hundred thousands of dollars into millions, but many of them lost most or all of it because they did not have an exit strategy (or were greedy). It is important to consult a professional and expert financial planner that you can trust for help.

6. Diversification of Investments

Diversifying your investments (commodities/utilities/energy/finance etc.) reduces your risk. The goal is to minimize losses and maximize returns, but remember that the higher the return, the greater the risk.

7. Home Ownership: Renting vs. Owning

Consider a 25 year span. From the premise of costs alone, during the first 12 years the renter would pay on average about $250/mo. less but due to inflation would pay on average about $550/mo. more for the last 12 years. Therefore on a cost basis alone, over a 25 year period, renting is more expensive than owning. However with home ownership you also get the potential for capital appreciation of the property.

In the larger centres, homes have increased in value on average between 7 and 8% per year over the last 50 years. There have been ups and downs, but the climb has been steady overall. Over a 25 year period, a $250,000 home today appreciating at 7.5% compounded annually would be worth $1,600,000!

So if you rent, not only are your expenses higher over a 25 year period, but you also miss out on the $1.6 million bonus! Even if the home were to appreciate only 5% annually, you would still have a bonus of about $870,000.

In your first few years, you may want to rent just to get steady on your feet. After that get something you can afford (1/4 of a fourplex, 1/2 of a duplex, or a townhouse). Condos are generally not recommended because of the condo fees. After, say, 5 years, a $150,000 initial purchase could be sold for about $212,000 (compounded at 7%). This would give you about $65,000 for a down payment on your next home.

Summary

In my consulting work with employees of small business owners the topic of finance always draws a significant amount of attention. It's a very personal thing and virtually all of the people I have worked with have a keen interest in this area. They want to know how the success of the business will affect them. Those clients who have implemented financial tools to assist their employees have, over time, observed improved employee commitment, energy levels are higher, and involvement has increased dramatically.

In a world where employee retention is such a critical factor to the success of any business an involvement strategy that includes financial benefits to employees is an invaluable tool. Wouldn't you feel more comfortable knowing that since your employees are involved in the financial success of the company they are not out looking for that extra $1 per hour somewhere else? If their financial house is in order they are much more likely to be engaged and focused on delivering results.

CHAPTER 10

Diamond in the rough

What follows are a few words from Dwayne Neustaeter, a small business owner who has successfully implemented the Diamond Solution and utilized many other of the tools mentioned in this book.

Do you put your pants on one leg at a time? Would you like to have more time and money to do the things you want to do? Do you want your business changed in a positive way and have happy, quality staff? Does the thought of creating a culture of accountability, profitability, and mutual respect in your business excite you? Then the Diamond Solution and the other tools put forth in this book are for you. These tools worked for me and they can work for you too.

When Neil asked me to share a few words about my company's experience with the tools and concepts he works with as a small business consultant I said yes before he finished asking me. There are defining moments in all of our lives that we'll never forget, and working with Neil on gaining clarity into my business has been one of my most powerful ones. These are special moments that you treasure the rest of your life and can point to with confidence as life-changing. I was thrilled to be given the opportunity to share my experience with you.

I can't thank you enough for taking time out of your busy life to read this brief chapter, as it is a small piece of my history that has become forever intertwined with Neil and tools like the Diamond Solution. I have found its unique view of business processes to be of enormous help in my business life, and my personal life. It has literally changed the way I think, behave, and understand. If you apply it over time, the Diamond Solution will undoubtedly have similar effects in your life.

First, let me tell you a little bit about myself. I was born and raised in southern Saskatchewan, where I grew up on the family farm. I used to love to go fishing as a kid and during the summer of my 14th year there was road construction going on near my usual fishing spot. One day I got talking to, and made a deal with, the on-site foreman. I ended up contracting my Dad's tractor to pick all the rocks in the mile and a half of construction zone. My intention that summer was to get my own motorbike and with that in mind I made enough money picking rocks to do just that. What I learned from that experience affected what I thought about business, success, and hard work. I have learned that much of what we do later in life is influenced by early memories and experiences we have as kids.

I graduated high school, attended the University of Saskatchewan, and went to study in Colorado. I was determined to start a family and have a business. By the time I was 25 years old I had started two businesses, sold one, had five jobs and gotten divorced. I still wanted a family and decided that I should get a career job, so I became a full-time teacher.

Later, I was happily married with a beautiful young son and had tenure as a professor at a college. I had it made—but somehow I was not satisfied and needed more. The answer to what it was I was looking for eluded me for a very long time. After many rewarding years instructing and many frustrating years of academic politics I started my own training company. I had met an influential person and was inspired by his organization and partners. I signed a license agreement in order to help gain exposure and start the new venture. My goal was to become an arborist training company whose recognition and business activities spanned the entire country.

After working diligently for seven years I had reached my goal—I owned a national, highly recognized, and well respected arborist training company. I now had two sons and my wife had become my business partner. I had what I was looking for—or so I thought. Once again, my wife and I found ourselves reflecting and searching. One of the most consistently frustrating aspects of our business was a lack of funds—something we now call profits. I decided I needed help and advice and in a moment of desperation I made a phone call to someone I had met many years before. This person was someone with a reputation, and people I respect respected him. I was struggling with changes in my life and business and needed an outside view.

My first meeting with Neil was at a restaurant over coffee. I have never been one to hold back so I proceeded to tell him everything that was on my mind. I remember him telling me that I was ahead of 90% of the businesses out there because I was asking for help. I asked for so much help that when I left and was driving home I was concerned that I might have scared him away. Luckily I had not. Neil then spent two full days with my wife and I at a retreat in the Canadian Rocky Mountains. It was here we were first introduced to the Diamond Solution. For the next year Neil worked with us regularly and I began to view my business very differently. It was like getting a new pair of glasses—I could see again!

Our business had developed to the point where we were hiring and developing instructors at an amazing rate, yet none of them were full-time and almost all of them owned their own tree care companies. As our training business grew we needed instructors more often and in order to keep growing we needed more students.

This is when I first started to view things with more clarity. Just like a diamond begins as a rough rock we too were an unpolished gem. I realized that my team needed to know what the plan was for our diamond and how they would be a part of chiseling and polishing it. I believed that until they realized the importance of their actions—one to another and with our clients—the diamond that was our business would never sparkle to the degree that it could.

I decided the best way to help them learn this was to have Neil teach them the Diamond Solution and give them a view of what my wife and I wanted our diamond to look like—how we wanted it to sparkle. I realized that what was unique about my company and its amazing people was that we were like a diamond ring, and each one of us would have to make the most significant contributions we could possibly make in order for the diamond to shine, and for customers to buy *us*. That is exactly what they were buying, us. If we were not in the business of serving our customers, and directing all of our energies into tasks that ultimately served them then we were all simply wasting our time.

After two years of utilizing the Diamond Solution virtually all of my instructors have hired Neil to work with them on their businesses, and some are even mentioned in this book. The diamonds in the ring of my organization are still getting worked on and we are all chipping away carefully trying to gain an even better understanding of our business and its sometimes complex relationships. With Neil's help and guidance we have expanded our business and streamlined many of our previous processes. With this kind of clarity into my business I now often ask myself why I didn't do this sooner. Neil and Able

Business Consulting have helped us polish our diamonds and made them much more attractive to the most important group of all—our customers.

I mentioned earlier that our business needed instructors and students. My view regarding students has changed also. Our company has specialized specifically in the practical skills of arborists yet so many arborists are also small business owners just like us. I believe that if arborists and tree care company owners were to focus on the business side of their companies and become better at business then they would need more staff and my company would have more students to train. Success breeds success.

Neil has brought terms like "assessments", "leaderment", "pragmatic value", "scorecard", and "Diamond Solution" into our everyday vernacular. We apply the concepts of negotiation and leading teams regularly and have come to terms with what it means to grow a business and get over the wall. We approach potential opportunities with more analysis and focus even more on involving our employees and partners in our ongoing development. Neil's impact has been, for lack of a better term, amazing.

> **Since implementing the Diamond Solution our revenue has tripled. Our internal company breakdowns and conflicts are easily detected, addressed, and eliminated.**

Our business relationship with Neil continues to grow and we continue to seek Neil's unique style of leaderment. The Diamond Solution has empowered my team and company to achieve results far beyond my expectations. Since implementing the Diamond Solution our revenue has tripled. Our internal company breakdowns and conflicts are easily detected, addressed, and eliminated. Our business functions independently and has been extracted and untangled from our personal lives. Neil has accomplished his goal by turning my wife and I into cheetahs in the business world. Neil, the Diamond Solution, and the other tools and approaches mentioned in this book have literally changed our lives, and they can change your life too.

Dwayne Neustaeter
President
Arboriculture Canada Training & Education, Ltd.

978-0-595-45571-3
0-595-45571-9

Printed in the United States
99634LV00003B/118-195/A